A Beautiful World

One Son's Escape from the Snares of Abuse and Devotion

By

Gregg Tyler Milligan

First published by Dog Ear Publishing
4010 W. 86th Street, Ste H
Indianapolis, IN 46268
www.dogearpublishing.net

ISBN: 978-160844-051-1

This book is printed on acid-free paper.

Printed in the United States of America

For [Spudie]. My son.

Loving him is the closest I've ever come to believing God lives in all of us.

INTRODUCTION

IN THE BEGINNING WERE THE LIES, those special little fantasies in the thousands that covered the bitter tracks the ugly truth left behind. The lies were my original verbal, mental, and emotional text. I worshiped them as one worships a savior for believing he protects his followers. And they did protect me through the patchwork pieces of what was really happening. When Mother beat me, or when I caught a glimpse of one of her many money-for-sex performances with a drunken stranger, I would lie to myself that she only hits me because Father hits her. Or, she sleeps with bitter angry men for money only because she is lonely and we are poor.

I lied in every word – to myself and everyone – but no longer do I have the right or luxury to do so. I am constantly reminded when I dress and undress, when I see the lace of scars cris-crossing my knuckles and down my wrist or hidden beneath the underside of my bicep where Mother's wild sloping arch of the knife missed its intended target, a young boy's throat.

Even then, it was clear that the most important thing in my life, the only force pressing me forward, was to live. I buried the pain whenever I could and struggled to master every whim of my abusers in order to manipulate the next terrible beating or sexual assault. I tested and strained against the very boundaries of reality in order to wrap myself into a cocoon of a child's imagery where superheroes and mighty angels existed and made perfect sense compared to the agonizing world in which I lived. So often I played around the edge of insanity, stopping short of losing my mind altogether. Daydreaming constantly and getting nowhere. I stayed within an extreme and deep mental sleep while the torment continued without end or remorse. Mostly, I sat and watched these wretched things done to me, feeling a dull shame, and spoke to no one about them. I saw myself as a pitiful thing and less than a speck to all those around me. I knew so many awful things that they did not know or want to know. There were so many vile acts done unto me that were beyond my powers of comprehension, and I such a small and stupid boy.

Here in this life as a child, there was only me and Mother, and I tried so hard to understand why it all needed to be so cruel, clambering through long days of why there were so many terrible people in the world. Never understanding all of it, but the part of me that knew well the appetite for survival and enduring pain found the reason to search for the answers and since then reach for the stars.

Often, and only when Mother was sure not to notice, I would look at her. Had she seen me, she would have been shown an untrusting pre-pubescent face filled with silent horror and disbelief. In time, a terrible picture would form in my mind. There became enough proof, along with certain memories that would not stay buried, to finally show me all I needed to see.

Therefore, I write this book to focus on the acceptance of life as it is – in its ugliness and beauty. For triumph out of the loneliness of the individual, drawing on memories of the real inhabitants of the world in which I once lived and died. Thus, building a new world (*A Beautiful World*), where there are those who put the highest value on courage and love. Not the fittest survive, but the courageous. Those of us who will never quit.

Therefore, I have returned to the setting of my childhood, one that I have never left behind, but carried with me like a heavy stone – a stone that takes the form of ritualistic tics I still cannot shake, recurring nightmares that leave me nauseous and quietly weeping when I awake, and anxiety that leads to endless visits to emergency rooms and therapists.

And before setting down this stone, there is first a bitter and terrible tale that must be told. It is riddled with futility, extraordinary pain, and not one but many miracles.

If not for the reason that I can no longer lie about what really happened, then no other reason worthy. Except if you find some meaning in what I write, to buckle-down and bear the ride that takes you through your own hell, then that alone is the most important reason there is.

If so, please also know this – I am with you.

PART ONE
Black and Blue Smile

"There are people who have an appetite for grief; pleasure is not strong enough and they crave pain. They have mithridatic stomachs which must be fed on poisoned bread, natures so doomed that no prosperity can soothe their ragged and dishevelled desolation."

Ralph Waldo Emerson

CHAPTER ONE

HEN A TEN-YEAR OLD BOY, I stood looking out a grimy window from a tacky house in Minnesota. My father would soon be here. Would he again crash the battered front door inward and rush past me, as if I didn't exist? Or knock gently while seeing me pressed against the dirty glass and smile – happy to be looking upon the face of his youngest son? My heart refused to accept what my mind already knew.

As I stood there, with my far-too-thin body half-hidden in old curtains that smelled of booze and cigarettes, my mother's voice shrieked behind me. "If that queer cocksucker is on his way over here, hell can't be far behind!" I briefly wondered what a cocksucker was.

My name is Gregg. My older brother, who now stands only a few feet away from me, is Carter and he's twelve years old. Somewhere within this small and dilapidated house, is our sister, Lynn. She's eight and most likely hiding in a closet and trying not to make a sound.

My brother, much heavier, almost portly, is my father's first son and properly given our father's name. He was much taller than I with greasy black hair that stuck to his chubby face. His eyes were piercing blue, like Father's, and the small of his pupils looked like rounded black onyx. Although he was only twelve, his fingers were thick and man-like. He was solid as a horse and street tough. His wide legs balanced a substantial torso, which was squared off by two broad shoulders. When he bent his head downward, his hair hung catching only a slim blue slice of one eye. With his fists balled, he wasn't just a striking image of Father – he actually became him. It made me quiver in fear and feel a terrible sadness deep inside. When he looked like this, horrible things happened.

In contrast, I was small and frail, hiding behind oversized glasses. My skin would go from alabaster to ashen gray within seconds, depending upon the mode of terror. Both shorter and smaller than Carter, I was meek with thin, dangly arms. I was awkward and broken down. My stomach was sunken to the point that I could suck it in and create a gaping hole flanked by two sets of miniature racks that resembled ribs. When I stood next to my brother, my slender neck appeared better fit for a young girl. Half-moons lay beneath my eyes, but did not quell the deep green color wrapped in circles of gold. I was a squat bony boy, shy and unsure of my surroundings, unlike Carter who was a self-possessed bulk of a sturdy young man ready to do battle. My brownish-black hair mocked my frame, a matted mess of wiry strands that lay flat and lifeless against an undersized skull. Carter was built tough and gave off shiny confidence. I was the picture of weary, soft panic and always plenty nervous. Carter was a death bomb, and I wanted to be like him. Instead, I could only envy his strength and wish for his power, while banging blindly against a world where big brothers like him were better equipped and had the muscle and might to prove it.

My brother and I had our youngest sister to care for as well, whom we called "Pug nose" or "Pug" for short, because her nose resembled a flattened button. Our mother came dangerously close to naming Lynn "Caboose," since she was the last child my mother claimed she would ever have. As it turned out, she would be the last child born to my mother that would survive.

Lynn was a fragile little girl with a penchant for relentless hiding – in closets, under beds, and wherever else she could find room. She was short, as young girls usually are. Black hair rarely cut covered a head much too small and framed her pale doll-like face. Her facial features were diminutive except for large green almond-shaped eyes.

There could be little doubt of her mood. When happy, she would form a perfect "O" with her small mouth, pulling her nose downward until it nearly disappeared and took on the shape of a tiny button. Her teeth were a jagged row of miniature Chiclets when she laughed. When sad or frightened, she would press a mangled and worn blanket against the side of her face and suck her thumb. It was a habit she broke years before, but recently had taken up again during times of distress – and therefore, a habit that would take years to break.

Carter and I stood and looked out at the empty driveway. My brother shifted on his feet, still peering out the window in anticipation, and his breath made round steamy circles on the cold windowpane.

After he moved out, Dad would come back from time to time. It was to check up on what Mother was doing, or *whom* she was doing it with, more likely. That is what I thought anyway. It rang true because he never spent much time with us kids, and whenever he was around, he wore an expression of irritation and utter disgust. There was never much talking other than an occasional grunt, which we interpreted to mean, "Hello" or "Get out of the way." Regardless, we never got to say much to him before he and Mother would start fighting, and when they fought, there was always blood.

Once my father arrives, it will break the trance I've yet again allowed to take hold and melt away the disquiet. I have two lives. As I look out the window, standing rigid with my fists clenched under my chin, I think of both of them. One life is made up of heroic fantasies. Often of being a military hero. A high-ranking officer who performs brave and honorable acts of gallantry. Where I rise above abnormal conditions and always triumph. I was the best in my unit and the one called upon for the difficult missions.

The other life is nothing short of arid torment. A barren and waterless place detached from God. A life where I am not fierce, but clumsy and thin and subjected to coarse decadence. Brutal betrayal rains down on me daily. I am insignificant and have never known true courage outside of my incredible fantasies.

The fantasies are my shield against the savage secrets that sometimes creep into my mind, bringing me dangerously close to insanity. Underneath these childish daydreams is only a thin veil of protection. I have honed the ability to slip into a well-timed fantasy at the speed of light. Moving delicately between fantasy and reality and down a magical well guarding me against evil – this allows me to glide quietly away from the anguish of abuse. Sensing any danger, I am always within reach of this power. It is my only source of life.

In the darkest depths, I need these two lives, even though the one that promises of comfort and security is unreal. Without it, I am left with living the reality of a nightmare.

"Dad's here!" I jumped when my brother yelled, and my mother came running into the living room. Her hair was primped and pulled back with a colorful band, and she wore a deep red lipstick. The desperate effort put into hiding the effects of alcoholism were obvious and only because Father was coming over. Otherwise, she rarely, if ever, gave much thought to personal hygiene. Mother would seldom brush her teeth, comb her hair, or even bathe. A repugnant habit adopted by her children as well.

Mother was no longer stunning, at least not like she was in her younger days when she had been voted prom queen by the senior class of her high school. I knew very little of Mother, having only gleaned bits and pieces through several thunderous fits of drunken rage and what was told to me by my siblings. Her name was Elizabeth, and she was the last of eleven children. Mother was once something special – referred to by some as a squaw, because of her American-Indian-like beauty. A beauty normally only possessed by Northern women. A dark exquisiteness. She had once been a waitress, kitchen maid, and wife of three former husbands. She grew up in St. Paul, Minnesota, and it was there she met Father at a dance. This was long before the alcohol stole her splendor, or before she simply handed it over without a fight.

Standing now in the living room, the difference was glaring. She had applied rouge to her cheeks, in order to compensate for the natural color now absent, but the fake blush did little to conceal the yellowish-gray of her skin. The flowered smock she wore hung much too loosely, and the low neckline revealed three grotesque bones protruding above the V-cut at the bottom. A pair of brown stirrup pants, meant to hug her thighs, sagged and bunched at the ankles, and I could see where she had cut off the cuff-straps. On her feet were old slip-on loafers without socks, exposing a web pattern of blue and purple varicose veins.

Before me was a woman I rarely saw washed or in clean clothes. Her stunted stick-like figure begged to be young again. By all appearances, her conduct was that of a beauty queen; however, all that was missing was the face and body to go with the confidence. I felt sorry for her and worried Father would find her ugly. The beauty had gone from Mother a long time ago. Left now was something small, wrinkled, and incredibly fierce.

As for Carter, Lynn, and me – we knew Mother as a wretched woman who never altered her plans outside the pursuit of her own selfish needs. We could always tell when she was angry. She made our lives unbearable, and her reasons for tormenting us were always kept a secret – but like those of a dictator, they were rigidly enforced. It was more than the alcoholism. Even sober, Mother was spiteful and full of hate. We never understood why she was such a monster.

When I was seven years old, she instructed me to strip down and climb into a tub of cold water. It was afternoon, and she and I were again alone in the house. I was always frightfully afraid of being alone with her, but could never leave. Carter and Lynn were outside and probably close, perhaps in the backyard. Within shouting distance, but it did not matter, because at that age, I would try very hard not to make a sound. I would endure Mother's abuse with obedient silence.

I sat shivering in the tub, with my arms wrapped around my knees tightly pulled against my chest. My testicles ached from the cold water, constricting something in my stomach and making it more painful. Mother took a cup from the corner of the tub, filled it with water, and poured it over my head. Gritting my teeth, I pressed my forehead against the tops of my knees. Still not making a sound, except for the occasional moan I could not help let escape. Even when the little waves of panic played around the edge of my dread, I remained quiet.

It was not until Mother wrapped her skeletal, cigarette-stained fingers around my narrow throat and began to choke me that I broke the silence. Hot urine ran from me and mixed with the cold bath water. I began kicking frantically, making rattling sounds. Upon letting go, I labored to drag the air down my burning throat. Coughing violently, black spots danced in the air before my eyes. As the air returned to my lungs, the black flecks began to slowly disappear, along with Mother, just as subtle and quiet.

While waiting for our father to arrive, I felt the dread creeping around my belly, and my brother's face was a perfect picture of what I was feeling. We both knew our parents were planning on a night of barhopping. And we both knew how it would end.

Carter had moved from his spot at the window and now stood near the center of the room. It was the vantage point he wanted when my father entered the house. I naturally took my place, off to the side and nearly hidden. Carter deserved the first contact, and if he were lucky, perhaps our father would tussle his hair, or better yet, pick him up and render a giant bear squeeze. Neither would happen.

Carter's excitement would peak while waiting to greet Father, only to be smashed into a million pieces when Father paid him little attention. Like so many times before, I would watch the whole thing play out on Carter's face. There would be this grin sneaking around the corners of his mouth, and his whole face would take on a special light. It was the same light I watched fade then slowly die when my father left every time.

Father was very handsome – in the old fashion sense. He looked like a comic book super-hero. His hair was black-brown, kept short in a crew cut, and he had deep blue eyes squarely set across his broad face. He had a rugged jaw and protruding cheekbones that made him even more striking. With his smooth shaven face, easygoing grin, neat tie, and blue work shirt, Father looked harmless – even passive. However, we knew differently. We knew he was sudden death. A horrific battle. A calculating man capable of murder.

His children were incredibly afraid of him, and when she was sober, so was Mother. There was good cause to fear our father. He had a short fuse and was violently sadistic. In addition, Father was six feet and thick all over except his gut. His upper and lower torso were substantial and made strong from high school football and years of manual labor while working on the coast survey. He had a wide neck that looked like you could bend pig iron around it. His fists were like bowling balls, and I saw them split the facial skin of both strange men and Mother with one wet popping blow.

Tonight our father entered the house, not with a crash but more of a sheepish lumbering. "Hey, Carter" was all my father said. He then made eye contact with our mother, motioned it was time to go, and left the house.

Mother passed Carter with barely a notice and swung open the battered screen door. Halfway inside and out, she turned and looked at me. "Find your sister. She's run off again, and I'll be damned if I'm going to waste my time looking for her." Mother then left the house, and with a bang of the screen door – long missing its hydraulic arm to ease it slowly shut – she was gone.

Once the house was quiet, Carter and I began to cry. My brother looked at the door where our father had stood only seconds earlier. His eyes were pleading with the memory of an image, dreadfully trying his best to make Dad reappear.

"He's not coming back," I said.

"Fuck you, Gregg."

I thought this last remark would be followed by a slug in the arm, but instead Carter only stood there. Dad would come and go, but my brother and I never did ask where he was going when he left, because we were sure it was always some place he would not say. Likely he was heading back to be with one of his new girlfriends, or to the Alibi Tavern, his favorite drinking hole. There was something about his shrewd way of answering our questions which stopped us from prying. There was also something else; we undoubtedly knew that he just did not want us to know.

I loved Mother, but I worshiped Father. If not for his stiff and impervious exterior, which commanded respect, then most assuredly it was his unyielding quality of something cut ruthlessly from steel. He was vicious to his wife and insensitive to the needs of his children. However, it was difficult not to admire him. He dwarfed everything in his way, and in the afternoon sun, I admired how he cast a long shadow.

It was starting to get dark, and out the window, I saw a neighbor man walking by. He was an alcoholic, like many of the grownups that lived on our street. It was a poor neighborhood and bad part of town. He stopped and stared at me, waved, and then started walking again. "Looks like ole Red is going to the corner store for some Mad Dog," I mumbled.

Carter didn't seem to hear me until he replied: "Fucking drunk . . . They're all fucking drunks." This made me feel a little better. At least he wasn't staring at the damn screen door with that lonely look on his face. It would appear that there was still some fight left in him. We went looking for Lynn.

CHAPTER TWO

OUR NEIGHBORHOOD WAS A CONTORTED dirty forgotten place where the low-income went to retire and die. The last vestige of humanity unwashed. Nothing but old refrigerators tossed out in yards and shacks for houses. Run-down apartment buildings where the hookers stood outside and would show you their titties if you honked at them. Broken glass everywhere, along with needles and liquor bottles. You would be right to call it all these things. My siblings and I just called it home.

At the center of this home was Mother. As long as I can remember, I was her caretaker. I would spend hours in quiet waiting, trying to stay close and unnoticed, at the edge of visibility. If I crowded her, I would pay dearly. I also knew that not being around when Mother needed or wanted me would only postpone the unleashing of hell's fury, which was worse. Therefore, I would lurk around corners and behind doorways, listening to her movements and waiting to lend a hand at a moment's notice. It was a worrisome devotion. A strong and ugly love.

It was not that Carter and Lynn were scrubbed clean of emotion, but the evidence of abuse affected them differently. They found it possible to leave her and I did not. We all discovered the blessed lull between the horrors of Mother's wrath. However, there existed for me some small comfort in knowing she was safe. When Mother was asleep somewhere in the house, I would find sweet relief for a short period, but I constantly checked in on her. My heart would sink upon finding her awake, and I wondered how my siblings could put Mother out of their minds so easily. I hated them for it.

Mother built a relationship with her children based on unadulterated guilt, manipulation, and violence. She used anything that would hold us within her power and replace the wholesome defiance in her children with fear. She told me on more than one occasion that if I told anyone about what went on in the house with her and me, she would say I was lying, and I would be sent away.

At night, Mother would wait until Carter and Lynn had gone to bed before molesting me. In the darkness – always the darkness – with no light or eyes upon her, she would take her liberties while I said nothing and did absolutely nothing to stop her. The blinds were always down, and sometimes there was moonlight that came in thin slits from the bottom of the dark windows. As the tormented moments went by, I would fixate on the horizontal sliver of the only illumination within the room. In that line of brightness, I would find refuge.

It is true I often wished I could leave the house with my brother and sister. And at times I would beg them to stay with me, but they wanted to go and play and be far away from the madness. It was not like that for me. Behind the curtain of my mind, I saw myself finding her dead, and the fear of that was worse than Mother killing me.

The conflict between taking care of Mother and taking care of me was something I did not question. It was more than a part of my sanity. It *was* my sanity. That is all I knew and all that mattered. It even felt like love, and my love for her was every bit as true as her sickness. I would linger and not leave her. I believed that without me she would die. And there were times I did truly save her from real death.

Once I found her gently slipping underneath the water in the bath. She lay motionless and naked. The water a perfectly still shining mirror. There was no vapor rising from the water, now cold, and yet she did not stir. The only remaining dry spot was a circle of flesh surrounding her nose and mouth, and I watched it recede as the water crept inward.

Groping frantically at her arm, I took hold and heaved her upward. She felt as heavy as a bank safe, and I could not lift her out of the tub. Mother was too slippery, and dead unconscious weight threatened to pull her under. She was like a drunken anchor. I knelt pressed against the side of the tub, and held her head, making certain it did not dip under the water.

"Mommy, wake up. Mommy, wake up!" I pleaded and shook her to the bone. I shook her until the water splashed up and over the side of the tub, soaking the floor and me. I shook her until she woke up. When she did, Mother pulled in a tremendous breath, and I could read the angry expression on her face. My heart was pounding so hard I felt it might choke me.

From the tub Mother took hold of both my wrists, and her mouth became a vacant maddening gape. Letting out a deep smoker's laugh that became a growl, she let go a grip of one hand and slapped me hard across the face.

She would have drowned, and I saved her.

I cannot say when the compulsion of living for Mother consumed my every waking moment, but I know that I cannot remember a time when it did not. The feelings of love were real, but Mother had also made an art out of manipulation. It was one of her most prized attributes.

Countless times Mother would hold a knife against her breast while I sobbed uncontrollably, watched, and waited in agony. The tears rolled silently down her cheeks as she stared ruefully at nothing. Not speaking. Just twisting the knife in her hand, carefully and deliberately aiming its point directly at her own heart, but never breaking the skin. I was squatting beside her, occasionally tugging at her free arm. She would apathetically slap me away as you would a fly. Sometimes loudly threatening that she would fall on the knife if I did not move away from her. Then suddenly Mother was finished.

She would drop the knife to the floor and simply sit down on the couch, calling me over to her. When she beckoned, I obediently did as commanded, wanting desperately to believe, but never quite trusting. Within moments, I would be flung back savagely, her hands slapping at my face, her mouth open – and in her eyes, the same quality of hopeless despair she had when feigning suicide.

After each fake suicide attempt, she would beat me for stopping her from going through with it. It was always the same. Imminent death was the plot brought on by an act of simply not having the will to live any longer. And me, running after her, squatting beside her, or pounding my fists against a door or window, pleading with her to stop.

But the choice to protect her was final. The choice not to fight back and resist her was final. It was not just because the beatings would be worse if I did fight back, rendering any resistance futile. It was also because I could not fight the very woman I chose to save. It made no sense to me, and the strength in which to do so did not exist. Even when her long yellow fingernails were around my neck, I would not fight back, nor would I run from her. Not when she opened her mouth and roared, and I was close enough to smell the hatred mixed with booze and cigarettes on her breath. Tearing loose of her violent grip, I would only back away, but never ran. Even when her sickness stole my sleep as the days passed, and I had only the lurid nightmares to keep me company, I would not leave.

Father did leave. He left when I was five or six, I do not remember exactly when or why. There was no fanfare or buildup. I came home from school one day, and Mother said he was gone. This was followed by a tirade of cursing and a beating for good measure. I suppose Father could have left after finding Mother with other men. Who cheated first was a mystery to me. Perhaps he grew tired of coming home to the house in disarray, his children not fed, and the surplus of drunks pouring in and out at all hours. Then there was the constant bickering that would lead to the terrible beatings Mother would endure. The stench of the unwashed marital sheets, which still smelled like other men, would have been difficult to overlook. Father may have justified his own infidelity by telling himself he at least took it elsewhere. He could have left for all of these reasons combined, or just one of them. I do not know.

Father was not a good provider. Beyond the fact he abandoned his wife and children, he did not pay child support. He did not supply his family with any type of food, clothing, or financial means whatsoever, though he made a decent living and could have easily taken care of his family. He squandered most of what he took home on women, booze, and cigarettes. Between one vice and another, he didn't leave much for his children.

When Mother would ask for money, his eyes would grow narrow and dark. He would refuse and say she'd just spend it on booze anyway. Sometimes, he would hold up his calloused hands and show Mother the cracked and worn skin from hard labor to make a point. I knew he could have gone down to the grocery store and filled the cupboards, but I kept this to myself.

Father would go on protesting and telling Mother he did not have any money. "Not after the goddamn government took most of my paycheck," he'd shout. "Why don't you get a fucking job, lazy whore!"

I had overheard enough conversations and arguments over the years to know a bit about my father. He was a man of relatively broad experience in the field of road surveying and postal work. After taking a job as a dockworker for an airline company, Father managed to work his way up to an office position within the freight department. He was even the city dogcatcher at one time and dreamt of running for city council, perhaps even mayor, but like many of his dreams, along with his children, he simply gave them up.

He was the son of a retired cotton mill worker who served proudly in the Marines during WWI. An honor my grandfather often said was lost on my father who had not served. He and his father were never close, but they had quite a bit in common. They both were brutal and sadistic barroom brawlers who, despite their advanced alcoholism, never missed a day of work. They were mean drunks and beat their wives, but never their children. They were gruff and feared men, which they took for respect, and they both felt their lives and children had been an enormous waste of time.

Nothing moved Father to take care of his children. Not even the State could force him to pay child support. He felt such laws were there to screw the working man, and that the stipend the State wanted to charge him for support was plain nonsense. Mother would go to the Social Services Office and complain. However, since she would show up drunk, raging on about how the child welfare system was a total disaster, nothing changed. The people in the Social Services Office sat in tall chairs behind a tall counter and went about the business of doling out misery to miserable people. They moved papers around with slow hands and seemed lost in their own thoughts. Every now and then one of them would let their eyes wander around the room, fix on someone, and then they would shake their head in disgust. It was usually us they were fixing on when they did it.

What little money we had came from the Welfare Department and Mother's more disreputable activities. There were, however, a few occasions when Father would drop a quarter in each of his children's upturned palms. Afterwards, we sprinted to the corner store and quickly exchanged the small token for candy. Any gift from Father was eagerly accepted. Even when Mother threatened to beat us if we did. Of course, she never made her threats in his presence.

I do not know exactly why Father would come back from time to time. Maybe it was easy sex or a sense of familiarity. This had once been his wife and was still the mother of his children.

But it was bizarre to think he would take her barhopping. He must have known she would be parading herself in front of some of the local men she had been with sexually. Father would also have known that both of them became violently jealous when they drank.

Despite Father's shortcomings, Carter gave him infinite love; however, it was not returned. To simply not care, or at least not appear to, was a vicious quality of Father's. This affected Carter greatly, who sometimes looked at Father as though they had met somewhere else, in another time. It was a disconcerting look, and I could see that it made Father nervous.

Since Carter was given Father's name, it easily supported Carter's claim that Father loved him the most. However, the urgency to have nothing to do with Carter was evident.

Father's indifference to his eldest son did not deter Carter from pining for his affection. He would sit for hours on the front porch waiting for Father to come back to the house and often Father would not for days. When he did, what excitement Carter had stored for his arrival was immediately dashed when Father paid him no attention. Carter would hide in his room afterwards and cry; sometimes his sobs were so heavy that simple breathing became difficult.

They never played ball together or went fishing. There were never any of the normal father and son activities. Serious anxieties regarding his affection for Father eventually developed into a full-blown reason to hate him. The love Carter felt for Father was abruptly carved from his heart and in time became hazardous.

Although it was the nineteen-seventies: the time of peace signs and Joe "Keep On Truckin," Sergeant Pepper's Lonely Hearts Club Band, PONG, Happy Days, and being cool – this was all gone for Carter, and until you are thrust into being a father to your younger siblings, you just don't understand the gone part. He was pushed into the role of protecting his younger brother and sister, and it must have been unbearable for him continually witnessing how badly he had failed.

Early on, Carter was always there, doing what he could to take care of me. He would linger near me as if lying in wait for Mother to attack, and she never disappointed. Before he had the courage to stop her from hurting me, he was forced to watch, helpless and frightened. Although Carter did not physically intervene at first, he never left the room. Instead, he stayed and begged Mother. He sobbed, pleaded, and prayed aloud. It may have been with Mother that I shared the worst and most decadent of experiences, but it was Carter who felt the crushing weight of the world as a helpless spectator. One who bears the burden of a terrible responsibility, but none of the authority or training to carry it through to the end.

My earliest recollection of when he did interfere for the first time was near Thanksgiving. I was nine years old. We were happy to be out of school and even more excited it had snowed considerably. There was a massive weeping willow tree in the field at the end of the street, and it was covered in a cocoon of white frozen powder. Carter, Lynn, and I carefully tunneled our way below the thick low-hanging branches. We were delighted to find ourselves protected from the world in what appeared to be a natural tee-pee of ice and snow.

While the three of us stretched out silently on the winter floor of our willow tree sanctuary, we forgot about Mother. It was actually warm enough to remove our ragged coats, which barely kept the cold out anyway. I do not remember how long we were under the willow, but it was not until the November wind boomed outside and the light began to fade that we decided it was time to go home.

I was the first to walk inside the house. I had no boots, only a pair of old tennis shoes that were once Carter's. I came in the front door with the laces of my snow-wet sneakers flopping and slapping the floor because I still did not know how to tie my own shoes. Mother looked at me, and her face fell to an exaggerated sadness. Her voice took on a droning undertone, almost whiny. I remember it well because it was how she always started out while building toward her violent outbursts. It would reach a climactic point, but by then I was already fighting for my life. My eyes left her face and fell to searching the ground. I thought of running outside and into the night. Into the wet, dark snow.

Mother walked over to the couch and sat down, crossing her legs slowly. "I don't appreciate *(coming out appreechhate)* you kids being gone so long," she slurred.

Her movements were deliberate as if she were a guest at a royal dinner party. Carter and Lynn were standing behind me, just inside the door. It was now dark outside, and Mother instructed Carter to turn off all the lights in the house. The only light remaining was a lamp sitting on an end table near Mother's head. It cast a yellow glow against her face, and her cigarette smoke rose up and disappeared under the stained and dented shade. Dust particles floated downward from underneath the lamp. Mother sat smoking and staring right at me. When she took a drag on her cigarette, its ember glowed and cast a blood light over her face.

Carter returned to where he was standing, behind me and in front of Lynn. Mother crushed out her cigarette, stood up, and walked over to where the three of us were. Looking at me, she then put her finger to her lips and said, "Shhh, now be still." The expression on her face never changed as she shoved me backward. It created a domino effect, slamming me against Carter and Carter against Lynn. All three of us fell against the screen door and out onto the porch, where we went skittering down the icy cement steps. Lynn began crying immediately. Both Carter and I helped her up. Having no place else to go, the three of us walked back into the house.

Mother was just inside the door. She told Lynn to go take a bath and Carter to sit down on the couch. I would remain standing near the door. We all did as we were told. When Carter sat down, Mother turned to me, again her expression never changing, and put her hands around my throat. I could hear myself making thick sounds when I began to choke. The inside of my mouth tasted like pennies, and I made quick furious motions while grabbing at her wrists trying to free myself. This time, Carter was no longer simply begging Mother to stop. He was making her.

His hands were now over mine and pulling as well. The three of us were standing together – clenching, with Mother's hands around my throat, my hands around her wrists, and Carter's hands around mine.

Carter screamed, "Mom! No!" – and then to my amazement, released one of his hands long enough to lay a wallop of a backhand across Mother's face. She went reeling backward, breaking her grip. I was immediately filled with sweet air – along with a deep adoration for my brother.

While I was buckled over, fighting desperately to refill my starved flattened lungs, Carter and I watched with curious nonchalance as Mother slid down the wall she hit. She eventually came to rest, splayed out on the dirty living room carpet. She was not unconscious. Instead, only surprised and laid there blinking in the semi-darkness of the room.

Carter pushed open the front door, letting in the cold air and making it easier for me to breathe. Mother continued to lay there and look around the room confused. We saw with a tad of concern that her left ear was bleeding.

I would later suffer the consequences of Carter's heroism. This is why Mother began waiting until he was gone before unleashing on me whatever fancy of madness struck her. However, that night Carter proved to me and himself that he was a true giant, and we both believed in our hearts – to Mother as well.

The endless laborious task of watching out for both Lynn and me gradually took its toll, and Carter was forced to choose whom to protect. He must have been horribly sickened by the difficult decision he had to make. He did the only thing he could, protect our youngest sister by taking her from the house as often as he could – thus, leaving me alone with Mother, as I would not go.

Sometimes, Carter would come home to find the aftermath of his decision. His younger and only brother curled into a ball of agony and lying on the bumpy linoleum kitchen floor. My tattered underwear pulled partway down, exposing the half-moon shapes of Mother's nails that had bit into the soft skin of my buttocks only minutes before. Further reminding Carter he was just barely too late was the thick smell of urine, sweat, and alcohol that still hung in the air.

He would kneel over me weeping, and I could feel the weight of his shaggy hair on my face. I would hear the click in his throat while he sobbed, squeezing my hand tightly. Carter would raise his head to Mother, angry and pleading. At times, he only stared at her and into those dead black eyes. Other times he would shout hoarsely, "Why don't you just leave him alone!"

Lynn would be in the background, screaming as well. A sound too large for her small body. Her tiny mouth gaping, making a lower-case "O." Mother would raise her hand to hit Carter and then lower it. She then would walk away, and we could hear the sound of her collapsing onto the living room couch. As a means of insane justification or to lay blame, we would hear her from the other room, her voice dry and flat, "I told you kids to stay inside."

When Carter's eyes met mine, they would be filled with bitter remorse. There was also something else that passed between us, as it had during the countless other times he found me much too late. When my crotch had been dark with piss, the putrid smell of my own shit filling the room, still spitting out globs of blood – it was as clear as Mother's insanity – what passed between us was life and death.

Lynn, being the youngest, often found herself pitched to the side and forgotten by everyone. Carter was disinterested as older brothers are. It was enough for him to just get her out of the house. I stayed as close as possible, but I had Mother to care for. Mother herself was pitifully indifferent to her youngest daughter's needs.

Lynn had once made a trip round the block on her bike. By the time she came peddling up the sidewalk outside our house, she was in a full panic. She jumped from her bike while it was still rolling and ran inside. A terrible thing had occurred to her halfway around the block. She suddenly did not recognize any of the houses and began to fear that, when she turned the corner again, she would be lost for sure.

Watching Lynn was a heartbreaking experience. You could see qualities of immense joy she consciously kept in check. A picture-perfect young lady without any physical affliction, aside from the inability to say her R's, making her even more lovable. Evident in all her characteristics was a perfectly resolved innocent little girl's way of thinking. However, this was shattered, leaving only the bitter cries of a lonely child.

The abuse Lynn received was not physical torment; instead, it was sexual. It had not been Mother's better nature that kept her from beating Lynn; instead, it had been Mother's worst nature that would rise to the surface, and Lynn as well would not be spared.

Carter and I slept in the same bedroom and in the same bed. Lynn had her own bedroom, and a thin wall separated it from Mother's. Lynn's room was directly across the narrow hallway from the one I shared with my brother, and from where I lay on the bed, I could see both her doorway and Mother's. On some nights, I would see Mother leaving her room and going into Lynn's. Mother would try to remain silent while waking her. It did not matter because I could see perfectly how she would lean over the bed, removing the covers and whispering something into Lynn's ear.

Mother would then take Lynn in hand and lead her out into the hallway, making a sharp turn to the right and into her own bedroom. I watched as Lynn went quietly and saw her facial expression was always tired and sad. The springs of Mother's bed would squeak when they crawled onto it. Sickening anxiety filled me, knowing what I would hear next. The rustling of bed sheets followed by the snap of Mother's elastic band around her underwear as she pulled them down. Not wanting to hear any more, I would bury my head under the pillow and climb frantically toward sleep.

What little protection Lynn had from the beatings was lost in these bitter experiences and the endless neglect. Based on the normal instincts of a young girl, Lynn looked for direction from her only parent. What she received was the uninterested reflection of a woman who had no desire to be a mother.

Often, if I did not remind her to use the restroom, Lynn would soil herself. Without the proper attention, she would occasionally end up with a terrible rash on her genitals. Having no one else to care for her, and being too young to care for herself, I would have to administer first aid. Finding old creams under the bathroom sink, I would give instruction on how I thought they should be applied. It was embarrassing guesswork and a parent's responsibility.

I fed Lynn when I could. When I would often steal food for myself, I always made sure to take something for her. Although the apple tree in the backyard or the field at the end of the block was my private refuge, I shared them both with Lynn. She would sit next to me, usually a leg touching a leg or her arm resting against my side. Lynn understood the quiet and enjoyed it as much as I did. What protection and shelter I could give her, I did. However, it was limited by the constraints of my own frailties. Like Carter, I sometimes had only enough strength in order to survive and care for myself.

Lynn had a reflective temperament, but it was frequently overshadowed by anxious concerns that we were always about to be harmed. As a result, she would cling to me or my brother and warn us against an impending doom. She did not cling to Mother or trail behind her like most little girls. Perhaps she knew even then, the impending doom was Mother herself.

Carter and I had to become her guardian and neither of us were prepared for fatherhood. We were children, and the only examples we had were the unsettling observations of two parents possessing abusive characteristics. We were poor excuses for caretakers, and Lynn was abandoned, suffering the ravages of carelessness and no one to help her.

Carter, Lynn and I had four older sisters. By the time I was ten, they had all systematically moved out – escaped. The two oldest half-sisters, Jessica and Lauren, had married the first man that came along and asked. Ashley was living with the boyfriend who impregnated her, and Madison, for the time being, lived with Jessica. It was a temporary arrangement and the best she could do on short notice. When the older siblings took themselves out of the picture, with them went the protection we once had.

Lauren, the oldest, was in her early twenties and on the very few occasions when I saw her, she already looked much older. She was slim, tall, and always brooding about something. She did not look like any of us and had none of the physical characteristics passed down from a mother we all shared. Her hair was platinum blond and kept short. Her appearance matched her clothes, which were always screamingly clean. Her eyes were unfriendly and when she looked at me, I was frozen on the spot.

Two years younger than Lauren and hard as nails, that was Jessica. She drank, smoked, cursed, and could whip a whole lot of ass whether it was a man or woman. Jessica could "knuckle up," as the saying goes, and she relished in it. If she were drinking in a bar, which she often was, and a fight broke out, it was Jessica who probably started it. When she was in her early teens, she was short, squatty, and pleasingly round. At eighteen, she looked to be assembled together with just the right amount of smooth, compact curves. With one exception, she had a big behind that earned her the nickname *bubble-butt*. Jessica also did not look, or act, anything like Lauren. Especially when comparing Lauren's eerily controlled temper, long slender frame, and flat almost non-existent buttocks.

Jessica took to alcohol early on and drank so much that slurring her words became a natural part of her vocabulary. She often had blood seeds in the corner of her eyes from either leaving a hangover or working like hell to prepare for the next one. Like Lauren, she kept her hair short. It was a reddish auburn and brought the brown out of her beautiful, almost perfectly round eyes. However, when she drank her eyes were pretty no more and looked exactly like Mother's. And when she wore her hair a certain way, she even looked a little like Mother too, and often she had the same nasty disposition.

Still, there was also this other sweet side of her that came out sometimes. You had to catch her in those sweet moods, which usually occurred right after she had a couple sips of wine. However, a few more sips and she was yelling at you about being too loud.

I loved Jessica even if she did scare me sometimes. There was this time I had started choking on a jawbreaker while playing down the street, only a couple houses down from where we lived. I started to gag and immediately ran home. By the time I reached our yard, the world was going black. Jessica was there and just about ready to pull her car out of the driveway. The next thing I remember, she was holding me over the sink with her finger down my throat. I coughed up the jawbreaker and took in huge gulps of air. When the danger subsided, I started to cry. Jessica held me as my head rested on her shoulder. Rocking me back and forth, she just kept saying, "It's okay, baby – it's okay." It was easy to love someone like that.

Ashley was six years older than me, and when she lived at home, she did her best to protect me from Mother. Her defiance was a harsh tax on Mother's convictions. One evening in an outrage, Mother went after Ashley in a drunken frenzy. Ashley drew a knife she had pulled from the kitchen drawer and held it to Mother's throat. That was the end of Mother's attacks against her. Ashley left for good the next day.

Rebelliousness was inherent in Ashley's nature. It was as if she came into this world to discourage all fools. She seemed to possess endless courage, and it filled me with both dread and amazement. I admired her strength and loved her so much that I would think breathtaking thoughts about her, turning them repeatedly in my mind.

She was a natural beauty. Her thick auburn hair was combed straight down past her shoulders, and she often wore it pulled back with a headband. The first thing you would notice were her eyes. They were sharp and glinted when the light touched them. Adding to their unique beauty was the fact one was green and the other blue. Her nose was thin and perfectly narrow at the point. She had a doll's mouth, full and soft. Although Ashley was barely sixteen, her body was that of a grown woman.

Ashley would become pregnant soon after she moved away to live with a boyfriend. She would carry the child full-term, and regardless of Mother's protestations, she would keep the baby. At first, she wearily considered an abortion. Alone, she pondered this choice endlessly. There was no parental guidance. Mother had mocked her, ironically calling her a whore. According to Mother, it was yet another act of defiance brought against her personally, as if Ashley got pregnant out of spite.

And finally there was Madison. Madison had left in a hurry, as they all did and for the same reason – Mother. In one of the last terrible arguments she would have with Mother, she packed what she could and ran. I watched Madison go, and I wept, but did not ask her to stay. Even then, I knew it would have been unfair to do so.

Madison was two years younger than Ashley and four years older than me. Her mouth at one time had been almost voluptuous, but habitual muscular tension had drawn it close and made a deep line on each lip. She was still very pretty with long brown hair often tied in a ponytail and short with mild curves. Her eyes were dark, almost black, and they shimmered when she laughed. Her face was eager and mature for such a young girl and bore the high cheekbones of a native Indian. Her ears were much too large for her head and at times would poke through her hair. Their pale color would contrast sharply against her dark hair, making you notice them even more. She had small hands, almost too small for her body, and they moved graciously like those of the blind. I remember her hands while holding me on her lap. I remember that the most about Madison.

With our sisters gone, and Mother to deal with, our lives were not like most kids', but there were a few children in the neighborhood with whom we made friends. The Jacobsons, who lived directly across the street, had three children our age and gender. Kyle was my good friend, Louis and Carter buddied up, and Lynn befriended Alexis. Although Mother, her madness and my need to stay near her, prevented frequent interactions with the Jacobsons, they gave us all brief, desperately-needed moments of childhood play.

School however was a different story. In the fall, when most children were going about getting ready for the academic year, purchasing new clothes and supplies, I along with my brother and sister were mentally preparing ourselves for another year of humiliation. Somewhere hidden inside each of us, secretly waiting to explode, was the fear we all felt – remembering how we would be tormented by the other children. Our clothes were hand-me-downs from Goodwill or the Salvation Army and were never a good fit, either too big or too small. The trousers were littered with patches sewn on by their former owners. Every stitch was worn thin and stretched to the breaking point. The fabric was shiny with wear in places, and the shirts, dresses, and pants stank of stale cigarettes and mothballs. We looked and smelled poor.

Our hair was shaggy and unwashed. Our faces were often dirty, and mine was sometimes bruised, albeit lightly, which generally looked to be the result of innocent play with other boys. During the school year, Mother was always careful to hit below the neck, and she intentionally avoided the legs and arms. Occasionally, there would be the remaining bluish hue of her fingertips as a result of her choking me. Mother would use flesh-tone makeup to conceal the marks, and I was desperately afraid it would rub off and someone would notice. We drew no attention nor did we seek it. Confessing to a teacher was out of the question. If not for the fear of retribution, it was inconceivable to imagine divulging what dirty little secrets were kept hidden in the darkness of Mother's room.

Because of constantly wetting the bed, I often smelled as if I had bathed in urine. The odor emitting from damp yellow underwear hung to the crotch of my pants. The schoolchildren would point their fingers, laughing and holding their noses when I walked by. My siblings and I were relentlessly targeted when it came to the other children. They would tease us incessantly. We were easy prey. The poor always are.

I would sit facing away from the other children in the cafeteria, in order to hide as best I could the State-provided free lunch. Both hungry and humiliated, I would quickly gobble down the food. When the other children traded snacks, I could only watch with envy. Making it worse, from time to time a well-meaning lunch lady would take up a collection of treats for me. Reluctant children would hand over their pudding cups and sweet pies. Once laid out before me, I would greedily eat the vast array of colorful delicious snacks. They were scrumptious, but did not douse the bitter taste of shame in my mouth.

Academics were an afterthought compared to the basic needs of survival. We missed a significant amount of school. Mother would sometimes forget and think it was summer. My siblings and I never brought this to her attention. Instead, we would stay home, choosing rather to take our chances with Mother than face the humiliation of other children and the stresses of schoolwork far beyond our comprehension. We all fell behind and were below the recommended reading, writing, and arithmetic levels. At ten, I still did not know how to tell time or tie a shoelace. I would steal the homework from book bags and lockers of other children and copy the assignments. I cheated on tests – if I did not cheat, I flunked.

Each school year, the lessons became more difficult and the children more sadistic. Barely passing each grade level, we were more broken and no smarter. At the end of each year, my brother, sister, and I sighed with relief. We would find some comfort in not having to contend with yet another meaningless prospect of disgrace – one less reason to feel *dunce* was stamped upon our foreheads, no need to worry about readying ourselves for school after long sleepless nights. When summer finally arrived, it brought with it the chance to let the shame of the school year die away.

Summer also meant not having to desperately conceal my "tics" from the eyes of the cruel schoolchildren. My obsessions ran the gamut from constantly needing to get the saliva out of my mouth to touching and re-touching objects. I was also absolutely certain for about six months that I would die of a heart attack. I remember when it all started.

It had been with a film we watched in school about a boy my age. The similarities between the boy and me filled me with terror. His parents fought, children shunned him, and he was lonely. The film cut to a time earlier that morning and showed the boy's parents fighting. Later, the boy asks his father to play catch and his father refuses. The boy was already wearing his baseball glove, and I felt sorry for him even more.

At the end of the film, the boy boards a school bus. Minutes later, he walks to the front of the bus and asks the driver to stop. He speaks in a low, almost inaudible voice that seemed to come from a deep and empty place. I sat watching the movie knowing exactly from where that voice came. The driver stops the bus, and the boy descends the steps. You saw his Converse high-tops, and then his ankles turn, legs buckle, and then he falls without a sound.

I watched, fighting back tears, while my anxiety blossomed. The film skips to a doctor telling the boy's parents that he died of a broken heart. The mother and father did not sit together. I noticed they were not holding hands. It bothered me a lot that they seemed not to care about what the doctor was saying.

That afternoon it began to build up inside me. The boy in the film kept weaving in and out of my head. It worked on me until I was convinced it could happen. The fear dragged at me, and I waited for the moment when I would die of a broken heart.

I needed constant affirmation my heart was beating. So, I ran from morning 'til night in order to feel the hard rhythm of my heart slam in my chest. As soon as the pounding subsided, I was off and running again. The worst of it was when I could not leave Mother in order to run outside. Disappearing into the bathroom or out of Mother's sight, I would press my hand against my chest and concentrate until I thought I could feel a beat. It was pure agony, but I still chose to stay with her. A choice I made easily when it came between Mother and me. Mother always came first.

Life was a long period of agony and waiting. We were hungry all the time. The food was scarce, and the kitchen was off limits according to Mother – who usually announced this with her belabored decree – "The kitchen is now closed." What little food we might have found in there would have been beyond consumption anyway due to aging, mold, or roach shit.

With this lack of food, we had to resort to stealing from the corner store. The store was at the end of the block, luckily within walking distance from the house. The storekeeper was a bitter, rotund Hungarian. His eyes glittered blue sparks, piercing out of dark caves. The skin beneath his eyes went blackish brown when he became angry. His nose canted to the left and was badly pocked. It looked broken and I wondered how he could breathe through it.

When I first started stealing, I would panic and stand there like I was frozen in mud, letting the storekeeper scream and cuss and get close enough almost to catch me. Later I learned the trick was to wear an old hat to hide stuff under, or pants with deep pockets, and just waltz right out of the store. In the winter, I would wear a big floppy coat, but that would not work in the summer.

Mother also frequented the corner store to get her booze and cigarettes. The storekeeper had everything crammed inside that small and crowded corner grocery. He sold what you needed or wanted, and that was what mattered. He even cashed paychecks and food stamps. You couldn't use the stamps to buy booze or cigarettes, so the keeper would let you purchase the legal items, *what you needed*, and you worked it out so you had cash money coming back. With that, you purchased *what you wanted*.

I went on stealing when I could, and the storekeeper never bothered to throw me out when I returned. He probably figured the money Mother spent was worth the occasional snack he lost. Things went on as they always did. The only time I was ever chased beyond the parking lot of the corner store was not by the old Hungarian, but by a bread delivery driver.

I had snagged not a loaf, but a whole rack of bread from the back of the truck. I remember the small parking lot had just been freshly tarred and lined, which had a sweet industrial smell to it. As soon as I took off running, I could hear the driver shouting after me. I was hungry – no, starved – and by the time I crossed the street, he was already gaining. The rack was awkward and difficult to run with, so I dropped it. Regardless, he continued after me. I tore down the sidewalk, my hair plastered to my skull in sweat strings with my arms pumping like mad. I could hear his harsh breathing and knew he was closing in. He wasn't yelling any longer, and I felt his fingers brush the back of my shirt lightly, making me scream. With a newfound burst of energy, I pulled ahead and left him far behind. I did not dare look back until I was nearly to the field.

The chaos of our home life suffocated the normal activities of childhood. Seasons and holidays came and went. Christmas was something trivial, unimportant and without meaning. I certainly did not have gifts to brag over the next day with my only friend Kyle. When I got back to school after Christmas break, I would always lie and say I got a truck or a BB gun.

If Mother felt the urge, she would allow us to put out the old fake tree Father had brought home before I can remember, or the Christmas Wheel. The Christmas Wheel was fashioned like an old desk fan with the same shape and size, but instead of a series of blades and protective meshing, there was a large round plastic disk made up of various pie-shaped colors that would be projected on the wall. The tree was store-bought and looked it. It was made up of several wire attachments supposed to be the limbs, and glued to those were artificial bristling quills painted white. Most of the quills were gone, leaving bare spots when the tree was assembled. The wire limb attachments would stick into three green wooden rods filled with holes. One of the rods was lost, so it was now a much shorter fake tree with a bad case of the mange.

We would turn off all the lights and aim the Christmas Wheel at the tree. It would go round and round, making this low throbbing noise. With the lights off it was much better, because you could not see how ugly the tree was or that it didn't have any decorations. When all the lights were off, including the Christmas Wheel, you could not see there weren't any presents under the tree either. That was Christmas.

There may have been Thanksgiving too, but I do not remember it. Therefore, I do not have any grief for what was gone because it does not stick in my mind as a memory.

There were a few winter experiences though that I can warmly recall. I would sometimes go skating with my brother. When we were skating, Carter and I were happy. We would go down to the fire station, pulling one another on a sled, and then strap on our skates and chase each other around the rink. The skates were hand-me-downs from older siblings. Often, I would be wearing girl skates which were still too large; however, newspaper made them fit.

The fire station sat on top of a large hill, which was great for sledding. Its steepest slope was just below three enormous doors, and behind the doors were the huge fire trucks. Below the hill was a sunken expanse of land that always flooded when it rained and made a perfect ice rink in the winter.

The fire station would use the thick hoses from one of the engines to fill the recessed area. Sometimes, Carter and I would watch the firemen prepare the rink. The best part was watching the hose stiffen right before the water came gushing from the end. The station maintained the rink, and the locals looked forward to its opening every winter, but not as much as I did. It was a safe place full of fun, and best of all, within walking distance from home.

We would sit atop the big hill that overlooked the ice rink and watch the other skaters go whizzing by, shouting at the neighborhood kids we recognized. Sometimes when the fire station served hot chocolate, we'd drink so much that our small bladders felt ready to burst, and we'd be forced to sneak a piss in back of the fire-red brick building. We would skate and sled for hours until our fingers and toes, wrapped in plastic bread bags, were frozen. But we would not go home. Sometimes we waited until the fire siren blew, signaling the rink was closing. The time spent away from Mother did us good. It made us strong.

The birthdays also came and went without parties or friends. There was a moratorium on sleepovers, what few we had from time to time, which was a blessing in disguise. During these painful few, Mother would always be involved somehow. She would force us along with our friends, which were usually Kyle, Louis, or Alexis, to sleep all together on the living room floor.

She would explain loudly to them that this was so she could keep an eye on me. Because she believed I would do the most atrocious things with Kyle if left alone with him.

Mother would then flop down in between us and promptly pass out. The last sleepover ended with Mother urinating and defecating herself while she slept. Kyle, who was asleep to one side of her, ended up getting some of it on him. He woke up feeling the wetness. When he realized he got a good dose of Mother's excrement on him, he started to gag, and then he puked all over the blanket on the floor. Mother kicked him out of the house and told him to go home. She cussed him out pretty bad, calling his mother a whore and said he could go fuck himself and the horse he rode in on – one of her favorite lines. Louis was there as well, and he left with his brother. Carter and I cleaned everything up including Mother, gagging ourselves, but we did not puke. Maybe it was because of all the practice; somehow we had gotten used to Mother crapping and pissing herself. Regardless, that ended the sleepovers once and for all.

Desperate, I thought once about trying to tell these things to the store-keeper at the corner store, although he hated me for stealing from him, so much he would throw lit matches at me and chase me away. I also thought about telling a kind-faced neighbor. I would tell them the whole story – even the embarrassing parts about the bad stuff in the bedroom. Nevertheless, I knew that if I went and told anyone, Mother would come and drag me back home, and the man at the store or the neighbors would let her do it. They were afraid of her. More than they cared about me.

I could not tell a social worker either. They only came to the house by appointment, and Mother would get prepared. Mother would mark the day and time on a piece of paper, and stick it to the front door as a reminder. She would make us clean the house, and then she would hide all the booze. Mother would open some windows to air out the smell of stale wine and whiskey, even if it were winter. If the social worker asked why it was so cold, Mother would probably tell her the furnace was old, and we could not afford to get it fixed. That would get her sympathy.

I had seen how Mother was good at playing people when she wanted something and how she could easily get people to feel sorry for her. She was also very good at telling people what they wanted to hear. Mother would be sick from not drinking, and I bet she played that up for the social worker too.

I had watched many times when, shortly after these visits, she'd be at the corner store buying alcohol and doubled over in pain because it had been awhile since her last drink. Sometimes people in the store would ask her if she were all right. Mother would tell them she had cancer, and they would get this sad look on their face. Then, she would be really pissed off because she had to wait and buy booze until the people she lied to left the store.

After me and my siblings were finished cleaning the house, we would be sent away before the social worker was supposed to arrive. Mother told us that if we came back before the social worker left we would, in her words, "Pay the price." That meant we would get a serious beating.

Therefore, we never came back until the blue car with the yellow city emblem on the door was gone. When the social worker finally left, we would come home. Before long, the house looked like it had never been cleaned, and Mother looked like she had never been sober.

I thought about telling someone all the time. Perhaps Kyle or Mr. and Mrs. Jacobson. I would tell them the whole story, but never did. What stopped me was not just shame, but fear as well. Fear of Mother.

Mother had made sure to provide me with detailed insight of the consequences. Not only would I be taken away, but I would be sent to a boys' home where the older boys would cut off my winkie. She also told me that they would make me put their cock in my mouth, and I would have to suck on it until the white stuff came out, and then I would turn into a queer for sure.

I did not know if any of this were true, but I knew Mother was not lying when she said I would "*pay the price*" if I ever told anyone. I knew that was real. As real as the tears rolling down my face. It did not make any difference, because before Mother's warnings, I knew in my heart that I would never tell anyone. I would continue to keep my grief and the truth silent.

CHAPTER THREE

As THE SUN STARTED TO SET, Carter and I were underneath the apple tree in the back yard, enclosed by its thick foliage. It was a place we could go when scared or lonely. It was also close to home if Mother needed me.

Carter sat down on an old crate smuggled from the corner store's dumpster. On the side of the crate, down one of the slats, was written in big orange letters: SUNKIST. On the ground, directly behind where Carter sat on the crate and near the edge of where the low-hanging branches met the earth, there was a mound of dirt. Stuck in the center was a cross made from two Popsicle sticks tied together with kite string. From the stains, one appeared to be grape and the other strawberry.

This was where the bird Carter shot was buried. The bird he hit with only one try from his *Super-Sonic-Slingshot,* earning him a "double high five" from his younger brother. Both nervous and curious, I remember running over to it, excited at the prospects of returning the fresh kill to my big brother – the hunter. Only when I got up close, I saw it was still twitching. As it suffered and lay dying, its yellow beak opened and shut in a slow-motion fashion that made it look like it was trying to speak. Together, my brother and I picked it up and wept as the blue-black feathered bird bled all over our hands, shuddered once more, and then died.

I stared at the dirt pile, and the thought of the bird never feathering another nest seemed peculiar to me. It'd be quite dead and stiff by now, and part of me, curious about death, wanted to dig it up and take a look. I thought better and gave up the idea. Carter and I sat saying nothing. We took in the quiet and sweet smell of apples mixed with lilac. He rocked back and forth on the four corners of the crate, and I sat down with my back against the trunk. He was staring out through a small clearing between the branches and leaves at the stutters of fading light. I was staring at him. The quiet was good. This too would be behind us soon.

There was a terrible feeling messing around in my gut. It wasn't anything unusual because I always felt this way. Well, at least since I realized what kind of family I came from. Poor white trash. Drunken parents. Abused. Neglected. Molested. Hungry; always hungry. The feeling kept tapping something in the back of my mind. I looked at Carter. Could he be feeling this as well? Something told me that he was.

Carter got up from his box and crouched down in front of the crawl space used to enter and exit the apple tree. He was busily picking at a callous on his middle finger; what Carter called "The Fuck You Finger."

"Are you going in the house?" I asked.

Carter replied, "Yep, and so are you."

Trying to sound as sarcastic as possible, I replied, "Just great." I was eyeing Carter suspiciously. After all, he couldn't catch me if I took off running. Although I was two years younger, I was thinner and faster. I liked to run. *If it wasn't for the malnourishment, I bet I'd be the fastest kid on the block*, I thought. I was still fast even up against the older kids, like sixteen years old, who were almost adults; hell, some of them were driving. It was a pretty big deal that I could outrun someone as old as that in years, who had a driver's license. And on more than one occasion, I had to.

"Do we have to go inside right this minute?" I asked. I wanted to stay longer under the sanctuary of the apple tree. Moreover, I didn't want to be in that house.

Carter looked at me curiously. "Hey," he said, "are you a pussy?"

"No," I said. "But you're a faggot."

Carter was already pushing past the branch when he called back to me, "Come on, pussy; we gotta go find Lynn."

I was at a loss. It wasn't that I had forgotten Mother's instructions to us as she left for the bar that we had better find our little sister. It was that I was in disbelief. Here it was, the first time we get some peace and quiet with Mother out of the house, and Carter wants to go looking for Lynn, who's probably hiding under a bed and playing with her dolls. None of her dolls had any clothes anyway because they were lost after Carter and I stripped them all down and made 'em screw like real people. I never told Carter this, but I'd get a pretty mean boner when rubbing the smooth crotches of the boy and girl dolls together. What really gave me a weird feeling in my groin was when the girl doll had nothing on but a little skirt and I'd lift it real slow, like 'round the backside.

I was still too young to know how to masturbate or what in the world it was in the first place, but I liked the feeling the whole ordeal gave me. It wasn't like being with Mother when she'd make me hard by flicking it with her thumb and forefinger. Then she'd get angry that I was and hit me in the stiffness with the back of her hand. She would grab my hand and shove it between her legs, telling me that she's keeping an eye on my winkie and if he got hard again, I knew what was coming. I'd push up and pull back when she told me. Sometimes my hand would start to get sore. Sometimes after she was done, I would have to lie next to her and get poison whiffs of Mad Dog and cigarettes. I would fight the urge not to puke, feeling her pressed up against me. Sometimes against my groin – and I'd want to wash my hand real bad. I'd keep it down by my side so I wouldn't smell her juices, but I could feel them drying and getting sticky. After Mother finally passed out, I'd go and scrub my hands. It didn't matter. That smell would last for days.

When I got up to follow Carter, I saw something sticking out of the back of his pants. "Hey, Carter. What's hanging from your back pocket?"

He sort of reached around and felt his butt until he happened on the string hanging down.

"Oh, nothing," he said and then shoved the string back into his pocket.

I remember seeing something like that at Kyle's. The Jacobsons went to church every Sunday, and Kyle told me they were Catholic. They had religious stuff all over their house. There was a picture of Jesus on the wall in the living room, and another where he was eating dinner with his friends hanging in their kitchen. Carter and I sometimes went to church with the Jacobsons. This was one of the few times I felt all right about being away from Mother, but only for a short time. I thought the night service was the best. It was quiet, and there were less people. During mass, I would close my eyes and try not to think of the bad things. I always felt better in church. I felt safe.

I figured Carter had stolen the religious thing when he was over playing with Louis. I did not think there was anything wrong with stealing it. I sometimes thought of pretending to put money in the basket they passed around at church and then taking some out instead. Kyle said Jesus understood when people stole things because they were hungry or poor. I figured Carter took it because he thought it would help him.

"That's okay, ya know," I said. "I pray a lot."

We were now standing just outside the apple tree. I could see Carter was embarrassed. "That's cuz you're gay," he replied and started walking toward the back door.

It didn't mean much to me, what he said. I knew it was because he was ashamed. We were beaten for showing any sort of emotion. Once, Mother caught me and Carter holding each other, laughing and jumping up and down. We had gone on a coin hunt where we would find the loose change that fell from the pockets of the men Mother had over to the house. Carter and I would go on a coin hunt every now and then, and if we were lucky we found enough coins to buy a few treats. We would pool our money together and spend it all at the corner store. When Mother caught us dancing around, she slapped both our faces, telling us we were queer for each other. That was when she said we could not sleep in the same bed any longer because we would do nasty things. If we cried that made it worse.

"Let's go inside," Carter said again.

We passed under the aluminum awning that extended beyond the rear of the house. When it rained, it sounded like bullets and the spindly metal braces holding up the awning vibrated. I would put my forehead against them, and it would make my whole head buzz.

Carter said that lightning was going to strike the metal one day and kill me instantly. "It'll blow your stupid fucking head off," he'd say and then laugh really hard.

I told him: "You wouldn't be laughing if that happened – nope. You'd be screaming your stupid fucking head off."

It was no good protesting any further once we reached the back door. For a moment, there was hope when Carter hesitated. But then he grabbed my arm and said we'd go in the front door. I knew why he changed his mind, but didn't want to say out loud. Like me, he didn't want to be near the basement.

A bright lance of fear shot through me remembering when Mother fell down the basement stairs. In a rush, I suddenly remembered Mother near the top step, flailing with her arms trying to keep her balance and then falling. She actually reached out for me, groping wildly. Falling, bouncing, striking each step, and finally emptying on the cracked asbestos tile of the basement floor with a sickening thud.

It wasn't the fall that made me shriek in terror. That had happened too quickly to react. It was how her body laid twisted while still just inches from the last step. She lay ridiculously over to one side and near her head were pieces of bloody dentures. I don't remember running down the stairs, but I remember kneeling next to my mother, waiting for some sign of life. I remember thinking that the pungent odor of feces must have been the result of her extreme tumbling. Later, a brief inspection would reveal the odor had been coming from me.

"Don't leave me," I said abruptly.

"I'm not," Carter said, "but I should make you look for Lynn yourself while I go over to Louis's." The single moment of fear that Carter was half-serious passed when he smiled a bit at the end of his last statement. It was still no use trying to talk him out of going back into the house. I never really had a chance anyway; any opportunity that I may have had was now gone. It had dissipated along with the serenity felt only minutes before sitting underneath the apple tree.

"You coming?" Carter said.

"Yeah," I replied. We turned and walked toward the backyard gate in silence. The house gave off a deserted feeling, although I knew Lynn was somewhere inside.   Luckily, we had time to find her before our parents returned.

We were through the wooden gate and passing the kitchen window.   I looked at Carter, but his face did not change.   In the reflection of the kitchen window, I saw mine had not either.   Both of us looked afraid.

CHAPTER FOUR

A COUPLE HOURS LATER, after searching the house, checking to make sure Lynn wasn't hiding in her usual places, we went back outside and searched in the darkness. We looked in the backyard, behind the lilac bush and underneath the apple tree. We frantically walked up and down the sidewalk, past the neighboring houses. The cement was cold and hard beneath our bare feet. My brother tried running ahead of me, but was afraid to leave me too far behind so he doubled back, grabbed my arm, and we both ran back toward the house. It seemed like a long time had gone by. I wanted to scream out Lynn's name, but didn't want to draw attention to us.

We came back to the front porch, but instead of going inside, we cut away and ran to the side of the house nearest the driveway. This part of the house was dark except for a small illumination that spilled out from a low-watt light bulb burning in the foyer, atop the stairs leading to the basement.

The moonlight was enough to see the cheap aluminum siding that ran the length of the house, and I trailed my hand along its side for balance. "Watch out for broken glass," Carter hissed. "You don't have no shoes on."

Upon a closer inspection and more light, I would have seen the pitted remnants and small pockmarks left by empty whiskey and wine bottles that our mother had thrown and shattered against the house. There was so much glass strewn along the base of the foundation that, when the afternoon sunlight glanced off the jagged edges, it sparkled like pretty diamonds.

Carter looked in the backyard one more time while I waited by an old latch fence that had not swung evenly since the day my father attempted to install it. My father wasn't a handyman, and coupled with his drinking, even minor home projects never seemed to get done properly – when they got done at all.

Soon, our mother and father would be returning from another night of drunkenness spent at the Alibi Tavern or Mickey's, and it would be as bad as usual, but worse for me and my brother if we did not find Lynn by the time they arrived. They would be drunk and already fighting. And there would be blood and lots of it.

I needed to look through the kitchen window, so I climbed the squat wooden gate and stood on the quarter-inch slat below the ledge. It was just the right height. Even under my light weight, it creaked and groaned. The lip of the board dug into the bottom of my bare feet, and I immediately began to feel a dull ache work its way up my ankles.

We had checked the kitchen before leaving the house, but I wanted to check again. Regardless, looking through the kitchen window was an old habit. It was from there I could sneak a peek inside when checking in on Mother. It proved to be the best place to look for her. I was too short to reach the other windows with nothing to stand on. The living room window was low enough to the ground, but the curtains were usually pulled shut. And if she wasn't in the living room, she'd be sitting at the makeshift kitchen table. The kitchen was where she hid her booze most of the time, and you could set your watch to her needing a refill.

As long as I can remember, there were never any screens on the windows, and I never gave it much thought as to why. Lucky for me, because I would have had to deal with removing it, and that would give Mother another reason to beat me. She found enough reason already.

Pressing my palms just under the top of the window frame, I pushed up. At first, it did not budge. I pushed again, this time using my legs to push, which sent a shooting pain from the bottom of my feet all the way to my butt. There was a popping noise followed by a low hush, and the window slid upward. Just a crack, but that was enough to smell the familiar stench of lingering booze and rotting garbage.

In the backyard, I could hear Carter still looking for Lynn, who he thought might have slipped outside after we had left the house. I turned my face away from the kitchen window and caught a cool breeze. A bitter wind, my mother called it. But it wasn't bitter at all. It was very fresh and sweet. My empty stomach clenched violently. I had not eaten since the day before, and then it had been only a half-folded piece of bread with the moldy parts pulled off, smeared with what was left of the syrup. The cool wind blew again and brushed the long and unkempt hair from my face, causing me to close my eyes.

I heard Carter coming and climbed down from the gate, meeting him at the opening. His face was now very close to mine, and I noticed he was crying.

"I can't find her, Gregg. Mom's going to beat us."

Our father was an iron-jawed, powerful man, but he never physically harmed us. However, all bets were off when it came to our mother. When my father beat her, she would return the favor to her children. And she dealt me the most vicious beatings of all. Perhaps that's why Carter was weeping. He was thinking of what would come of me.

While we embraced, I felt the cool wind on my face again. Then I pushed away from Carter and forced a smile. "We'll find her. She can't be too far."

Carter shook his head remorsefully. "Well, we looked everywhere," he said.

Silently, we walked to the front of the house toward the porch. The outer search was over, and we needed to look inside one more time. We mumbled a little to ourselves and each other, but mostly shuffled along in silence. Carter muttered something about hiding as well and then said nothing. And then for a moment, we thought we heard Lynn crying in the house.

Carter cautiously ascended the cracked porch, and I followed close behind him. He stopped and stood directly in front of the door, looking at the lighted windows of the living room. It was a small house and Mother always said: "This ain't a home . . . it's a house! It's love that makes it a home!" She was right about that. This was a house.

We opened the door of the house and went in. Something was squirming around in my head, going round and round, and I tried to get it out, but just couldn't. It made me dizzy and sick in my belly. I had a sense of being in a waking dream, and a terrible thought rolled toward me: Lynn is dead, and that is why she does not answer. That is why she cannot hear us. I quickly pushed the thought away, but it was too late. The thought stiffened the hair on the nape of my neck, and a sense of lightness washed over me. The harder I tried to push the thought away, the stronger it came back. *Lynn is dead.* Just then, a bolt of lightning exploded in my head. All of a sudden, there was a sound I remembered, a smell I remembered. *Shit,* I thought. *Here comes the tick again.*

"The Tick" would show up whenever I was nervous; I'd start to repeat my words and actions until they ran their course or something else grabbed my attention and shook me loose. Most times, whatever snapped me out of it was worse than the rambling or constant touching and re-touching of an object. The first time this happened to me was right after one of my "day-mares."

That did it. Thinking of having what Ashley called an "episode" knocked the thought Lynn was dead out of my head and settled me down a little. Enough to pull it together and not slip into one of my walking nightmares. Good thing too. If I had gone on, Carter would have had to slap me across the face to get me back on track.

Just inside our front door, Carter took a few steps toward the kitchen. "Lynn," he called. "Come on! Answer me!"

We promised we would never tease her again, if she would just come out from wherever she was. No more making her drink out of the toilet or sticking gum in her hair. *Just please be okay,* I thought. *Please. Please. Just be okay.* Maybe Lynn just needed a little coaxing. Maybe, after all, she needed a whole lot more attention. Last in line and stuck behind six other kids had to be a tough spot. I suppose we just never thought much about how we were treating her when we all were stuck in the same miserable place. Maybe, after all, this house finally got the best of her, and she let it swallow her whole.

Then suddenly it occurred to me. "The attic!" I said aloud. Carter jerked back, as if I just smacked him in the nose. "Oh man! I ain't going up in that attic looking for her," I said with a noticeable quiver in my voice.

Carter looked toward the bedroom with the attic, where a dark square that hovered above the closet framed the opening to what we both swore was the gateway to hell. "Not yet anyways, but we might have to," he said.

Hearing these words made me squirt a dribble of hot piss into a pair of underwear much too large for my body and long past needing a good washing. Didn't matter. The piss would just be joining the many stains in the front and running a close race with those in the back rendered for much of the same reason.

There was nothing to protect us in this goddamn house. There were places around the windows and doors you could look through to the outside. Mother told us that the house had been condemned, which she said meant we were not supposed to live there according to the law. It was like bragging when she said it, but made me feel tired.

The house was an ugly ranch, a squat tacky square with a broken roof that sagged in spots and leaked. In the daylight you could see it lean somewhat, depicting a shimmering dilapidation. The cement steps leading to the front porch were broken, revealing tiny pebbles hidden under the concrete. In the sunlight, the house looked as if it was dying, and from inside, nothing was keeping out the wind or the fear.

Carter took in a breath, which startled me for a second, and I jumped to the other side of him.

"Cool it, Gregg! You almost made me piss my pants!"

I thought to myself, *Beat ya to it*, and turned away so he didn't see my cheeks flush.

"Lynn!" Carter yelled, and I jumped again.

"Let me know when you're going to yell," I said. He just gave me one of his disapproving looks, and I couldn't help but think of how much he looked like Dad when he made those faces. I bet if I told him, he'd find that a pretty neat compliment. Perhaps he'd work it around his head most of the day and turn it into something useful when the pain was real sharp and his heart was breaking all over the place.

"Lynn!" he called again, and there was a note of dumb terror in his voice. "Lynn! Lynn!" There was no answer. The house was empty.

Then, through the dank air stale from too many cigarettes, we heard the horrible sound of a child crying.

CHAPTER FIVE

I SWORE TO MYSELF I was leaving this place. The longer I stayed, I knew Mother'd kill me for sure. She'd hit too hard or strangle me for a bit too long during one of her drunken rages; my lights would go out, and I'd have only myself to blame. It would be my fault entirely. After all, I was the one that stayed behind.

The abuse was leaving dirty little secrets buried deep down inside me. I knew I wanted to learn things. I wanted to know what it felt like to look at the hands on a clock and tell what time it was or to tie my own shoelaces. I was tired of getting beaten for not finding her cigarettes, or worse, her making me do those other things. I worked so hard. I made every effort to say and do the right thing, which meant not pissing her off. And then there was how good I got at forcing a smile and the words, "I love you Mommy," right after she slapped me in the face or popped me in the scrotum. The breath gone from my lungs, but I got the words out nonetheless. The worst was pretending it didn't tear me apart to lie next to her after sex. The worst by far, but I managed to be convincing. So convincing, I started to believe it was my choice, and this was when I first started thinking about suicide.

I'd make a plan to get away. Not just me though, I'd work out a way to get Carter and Lynn out of here as well. It'd be a simple plan that would start out by getting a hold of Lauren. I'd heard she had a nice house somewhere in Minnesota and that perhaps she, along with her husband, might be willing to give us a place to live. Bring us in as sort of a charity thing, but at least we would get out of this place.

I wasn't real sure if Lauren would really take us in because that information was passed on to me by Jessica. She was one to drink a bit too much and had a nasty habit of squeaking a lie right out of a truth. Even if it was a lie, I didn't care. The comfort it gave me was more than anything I had to the contrary, and if a lie got me from one day to the next, then I'd take it.

Jessica's drinking made her an unlikely candidate for taking in me and my siblings. Jessica did not want us living with her anyway. According to her, with two kids already and a husband stepping out with another woman, she had enough problems of her own.

Getting out was the only way to save my life. I'd make sure I was a part of all those learning things I'd missed out on. I would study hard, fix on the tough subjects in school, and hang on until the knowledge was cemented in my head. At only ten years old, I knew things. Things that were going to help me survive.

Carter's head snapped back, as if he ran full speed into a low hanging branch. "Did you hear that?" he said, and then before I could answer: "That goddamn crying! It sounds like Lynn!"

I heard it all right. In no time flat, it knocked the recurring fantasy of getting out of this shit-hole of a life clean from my brain. We began to creep toward the direction of the sound, taking a few steps, stopping to listen for another shriek, and then bracing ourselves for when it happened. We were now where the edge of the short hallway cut into the living room.

A cool breeze was blowing, and it was too cold to have come from inside the house. In one of the three bedrooms lining the hallway, I figured there was a window either left open or broken – just about every mirror and window in the house was cracked with chunks of glass missing, which we were always cutting our feet on because we were usually barefoot.

I whispered, "Carter, I think a window's open."

My already small, prepubescent testicles, shrunken from fear, squeezed to the size of raisins when he replied: "It ain't a window. It's coming from the attic."

My mind rattled and I swore, for a split second, there was an old witch hovering just above the floor, only a few feet from me and my brother.

A few more steps down the hallway and we were just outside the first of the three bedrooms, the one with ceiling access to the attic. Carter picked up a dead cockroach that had squished itself between the base molding and the dirty shag carpet.

He examined it as if stalling for time and then flicked the infestation away. It hit the cheap paneling making a 'tick' sound.

Grateful we weren't going inside the bedroom just yet, I took the opportunity to catch my breath. It felt like a thousand needles in my lungs, pecking at my chest. I glanced over at Carter, who was hunched over, leaning against the wall. I asked, "Do you wish Dad was here?"

Tears came to his eyes. "Eat shit, Gregg," Carter said and once again looked toward the open doorway of the bedroom.

Still, no sound. Not even a peep. As a matter of fact, we began wondering if we had heard Lynn at all. We did notice that this was certainly the bedroom from which the wind was blowing. A quick peek into the bedroom revealed that the only window was shut, which further solidified our gnawing suspicion that the square piece of plywood covering the attic opening wasn't secure. We poked our heads in sync through the doorway leading into the bedroom, leaving our feet firmly planted in the hallway. When we crossed over the threshold separating the doorway from the hallway, the sounds started again, this time louder as if amplified by our acute fear. Carter gave a quick jerk of his head to the left, and I followed suit.

"Shit! The goddamn attic panel is slid over," Carter nervously whispered. "Oh man . . . she can't be up there," he said, as if to wish this whole scene away. The wind was blowing straight down from the attic. The panel door was slightly askew, creating a small pie-shaped opening that forced the wind to whistle. It was more like eerie singing.

Carter was now standing directly in front of the closet. The slatted folding door was butted up against the wall and pushed to one side. It had been broken off its sliding hinge the day Mother yanked it open – when she had found Carter and Lynn hiding in the closet and naked. Mother was furious and beat them both mercilessly, calling them perverts and incest demons. It had been all my fault.

Through the years, with each and every beating, between the incessant abuse and neglect, I would grow wiser. I would learn it was unsafe to trust Mother. That day would come soon, but it had not yet come the day I betrayed my brother and sister.

The closet had a step-up with a three-foot platform below a wooden rod for hanging clothes. We would pretend it was a spaceship. With the closet door closed, the sunlight would shine through the individual wooden slats, creating a multi-striped pattern against the interior walls and across the base in which we sat. It added to the fantasy that we were landing on the moon.

That day, Carter and Lynn were playing spaceship, and I stood outside the closet and convinced them they needed to remove all their clothes and give them to me. They did. I quickly hid their clothes under the bed and ran to get Mother. I had honestly thought she would find my silly joke amusing and we would all laugh. When she came bounding into the bedroom with me in tow, I began to realize my joke was going to have terrible consequences, but it was too late.

I stood with my back pressed against the far bedroom wall while Mother pulled my brother and sister from the closet. Their giggles turned to screams when the door crashed open. Our eyes met, and I saw the confusion and pleading glances from Carter and Lynn. Mother thrashed their naked bodies with a belt she had picked up off the floor.

My unsuspecting siblings tried desperately to protect their exposed genitals while the leather hammered away at their pink flesh. When Mother had finished, she turned to me. With only a slap across my face, she was gone. It was the one time in my life I had hoped she beat me. Beat me until unconscious, so I could pay for my sin and afterward know the familiar grace of nothingness.

From our vantage point, Carter and I could see into the closet and up into the attic opening. Through the sliver of darkness, I saw a small yellow eye coming toward us. It grew larger as it came closer to the triangle-shaped opening, and we took about four steps backward. I sidestepped to the right, and the eye appeared to follow me while floating just above the attic door panel. Its movement was purposeful, and every now and then, it would stutter crazily, slanting and tilting, and then right itself again.

"Shut up," Carter hissed. I did not realize that I had been moaning out loud. It pissed me off, but I didn't say anything. He too was making noises, muttering under his breath, and there was this low grunting noise coming from his throat.

Carter and I watched the yellow pupil move lazily from side-to-side – and at one point, it seemed to dip past the opening of the attic, breaking the plane between one dimension and the next. I thought to myself that this most certainly was an optical illusion and a very good one indeed.

Something moved just behind the eye in the attic darkness. It passed by slowly, moving to the left. I knelt on the bedroom floor, bending in order to get a better look at what it was. With my neck craned upward, I peered into the space above the closet. Neither Carter nor I was willing to get closer to the closet at this point.

"What in the fuck is it?" Carter said out loud.

I pushed my glasses up the bridge of my nose and strained to focus. "I don't know, but it looks like it's attached to the eye," I said.

My glasses were too large for my face, but they were the best we could do with the public assistance we had from the State. Being on welfare was our main source of income after Father left. Mother would get a monthly check along with food stamps. In addition, the State paid our utility bills along with the mortgage and we still had no money.

I remember Mother telling me that she spent over a hundred dollars to get my glasses for me. I knew it was a lie, but I would never correct her. That day, she went on about all the sacrifices made over the years for her children and the burden we placed upon her. It got her worked up into another frenzy, causing her to slap me across the face so hard it sent the glasses flying, leaving a deep cut over the bridge of my nose. She cracked the frames, but Carter glued them together with Super Glue. I remember him telling me that you want to be careful not to get the glue on your fingers. To add emphasis, he told me about this kid he knew that accidentally glued his penis to his hand. They had to cut some of his penis away to get it loose. That was a lie as well, but it was a funny story, and I liked it.

Now, in the bedroom, the light of the moon coming through the window lit up Carter's face. He looked worried.

I suddenly realized that Carter's hand was in mine. I must have grabbed it without noticing. Normally, Carter would not have allowed the affection and quickly flung my hand aside. He would then say, "You a fucking queer or somethin'?" It was more of an indictment than a question. Mother had often said I was queer. She frequently told Carter that he needed to keep a close watch on me because I was prone to engage in some sort of deviant sex act with Kyle. I wasn't queer and never knew where she'd gotten that idea.

The yellowish light in the attic flickered, or 'blinked,' and then went out completely. We could see it was real dark up there. Dark like the black monument with a black angel above it in the local cemetery. You couldn't see it at night, and when I ran through the graveyard one evening on a dare, I ran right into it. I busted my lip on one of the angel's outspread wings, and the impact cracked a chunk of it right off. It must have been old and crumbly like many of the statues. The end of the angel wings were thin as well and worn from years of weather. It could have already been cracked from me and Kyle taking turns shooting it with his Red Rider BB Gun. We must have peppered those wings pretty good – especially because we were only about four feet away. So close that one time a BB ricocheted and hit Kyle in the leg, which he said stung like a bitch.

Maybe it was just morbid curiosity or just plain stupidity, but I reached down, picked up the broken piece, and shoved it in my pocket before taking off again. I remember thinking the next day that when I died, there'd be an angel wanting his wing back. It spooked me so badly that I went back and laid it at the base of the headstone. I backed up a little to take another look, and that angel perched atop the headstone now appeared to be staring down at the busted wing.

Just then, we heard a loud thump. Whatever it was, it was moving and had managed to walk or crawl over the ceiling right above us. This got us going again, and we ran from the bedroom. About the time we hit the hallway and were soon to be out of the house for good, we heard another scream. This time, there was no doubt about it. Lynn was in the goddamn attic.

Standing perfectly still next to Carter, I waited for another sound. We had stopped in the hallway, both looking fearfully back at the bedroom. Long black segments of terrible thoughts clicked past just behind my eyes, and I thought of my recurring day-mares. The same feeling that crept into my gut right before I sunk into them was gradually gaining speed.

Fear always set off the memories, and they would trigger the goddamn day-mares. The day-mares, or episodes, began soon after the molestations by Mother. During the day-mares, my thoughts would roar by too fast to grasp, but time would slow considerably. I would run in all directions, screaming obscenities, climbing deeper into a delusional state of panic. There was a feeling of dull rage directed at no one in particular, but if my mother tried to grab hold of me, I would beat her with my little arms. Most of the time, I ran too fast for anyone to catch me. I would run as fast as my legs would carry me through the small house, and if I managed to make it through the front door, I would go sprinting away.

The episodes came not only during the day, but in the night as well. Occasionally, breaking free of my siblings who tried desperately to hold on to me, I would exit the house. Running past all the homes in the neighborhood, with the coolness of the summer evening on my face giving me more speed, I'd distance myself even further from those in pursuit. The anger and panic would dissipate, replaced by an overwhelming sensation of freedom.

Unaware that I was slipping further into the trance-like state of another episode, Carter was trying to tell me something. His voice drifted in and out, becoming nothing more than an echo losing its power after each consecutive repetition. The long black tunnel I was now tumbling downward was a sweet release, and I simply let it take over.

When the episodes first started, I used to fight them because I was afraid. However, as the pain piled up, I stopped fighting them altogether. Within the dazes, I had strength and courage. They were my blanket against a worn-out world.

I was now completely under the hypnotic stupor, and I no longer felt the pangs of hunger or bewilderment of what lie ahead. I was a super-hero. It caused me to make right what so many had wronged for far too long. My fury was so powerful, I could even taste blood. A thought came to mind that not only could I taste blood, but my mouth seemed to be filled with it. It was so vivid that I could even smell the iron and feel the congealed consistence running over my tongue and down my throat.

From what seemed a great distance away, I could hear high-pitched shrieks. Closer now.

"Let me go! Let me go!" The voice sobbed and whimpered, and with each cry for mercy, I grew stronger.

No, I thought. Louder yet, I could hear their shouts of pain and agony. It was a remarkable sound, and I relished in it.

"Let me go! Gregg!" With this last, something popped inside my head. The words were right, but the voice was all wrong. This was not Mother's demanding and impatient voice. The voice seemed to be terrified, pleading, and Mother never begged. "Let me go, Gregg! Goddamn it, wake up!" It was Carter's voice I heard, and with this realization, the episode ended abruptly.

I was suddenly thrown against the wall of the hallway, smacking my head hard enough to cause a great light to explode in front of me. As I continued to ascend the ladder leading from my fantasy nightmare, I realized that Carter was kneeling a few feet from me. He was holding his right hand over his left shoulder.

Carter then moved his hand from what appeared to be a wound and turned in my direction, looking only at my feet. "You fucking maniac!"

He barely got the words out, choking on each one as he did so. "You fucking cocksucker!"

He wiped away at his shoulder and I had a clear view of why he was bleeding. The last thing I saw before puking all over the front of my shirt was what appeared to be a clear impression left by a small bite. I had really clamped down on his shoulder. Mixed with his sweat and a small splotch of blood was an ellipse of tooth-shaped tiny red cuts.

When the sickness passed, I walked over and knelt down beside Carter on the hallway floor. He was still pretty pissed off, and right about then, all I wanted to do was disappear into the blackness of the night. My heart was still fluttering inside my chest, and I waited for Carter to really cut loose and leave me to deal with this situation all by myself. He'd done it before, many times, when things got real bad with Mother. He'd take off for the field down the street to hide out and smoke cigarettes with Louis until things blew over. I would tell him not to go – beg him not to – and he would just walk past me and out the door as if he didn't care about what was going to happen to me. I hated him for that and envied him at the same time. But right now, I did neither.

It was a hopeless ordeal for both of us. Any choice we made would end in defeat. It was a question of the lesser of two evils. When Carter would leave me, he did sometimes ask me to go along. I wanted to go with him more than anything, and I'm sure he saw that in my eyes. Maybe that is why he did not linger when waiting for my decision. Most times, he was already walking past me and through the door before my answer was even out.

I wanted to go with my brother. Even if it meant being teased by him and Louis or choking on a cigarette just to be accepted. I would have gladly been the brunt of their jokes, but we both knew that it was impossible. Just as Carter had no choice when it came to caring for Lynn and taking her from the house, I had no choice but to stay with Mother. Torn between staying and leaving, I chose to stay. Leaving with Carter, I believed, would have led to Mother's imminent death. A fate worse than freedom.

It was unfair of me to beg Carter to stay – to expect him to join forces and align ourselves against the common enemy of our mother. Of course, it was unfair, but it was an act of desperation. Descending upon us like an enormous hand and flattening our bond were the choices we both continuously had to make. To stay or leave was only one of them – and like so many other terrible choices we faced, it was slowly ripping apart our brotherhood.

"Carter," I said, "we have to get Lynn." There was no reply. Carter continued to sit motionless and stare at the growing drops of blood. We had to get going. It had been far too long since we first heard Lynn scream. Mom and Dad would be home before morning. The bars closed around 3:00 a.m., and it was nearing that time.

At the thought of our parents returning, my heart fluttered again. I put my hand on my chest to quiet the fluttering and waited for Carter to gather himself up. My head was filled with a hollow drumming sound, and I was scared to death not knowing in what shape we would find Lynn.

Carter stood up, and without further mention of the biting incident, he said, "Let's go." We walked back into the bedroom. The same bedroom Mother used to have sex with other men, when she wasn't using the bed Carter and I slept in. The same bedroom where I had laid down with her – afterwards just wanting to scrub myself clean, but not being able to do so – fearing the bath would have wakened Mother who was already stirring. Instead, I lay awake next to her trying not to think about what just happened. Trying also not to think about all the men who paid to lay with her in the same bed.

There were other places we would have rather been. There was the physical and sexual abuse, which was bad enough. However, Mother and Father were in the business of "Do as I say and not as I do." Mother made me out to be a sexual deviant, but then prostituted herself out to the neighborhood men and sometimes took care of business in the very bed I was to sleep afterwards. Father beat Mother for having affairs with other men, but slept around himself, which was what prompted most of their brawls. Mother would surge into every one of their vicious fights screaming about all the women Father had had sex with, and Father would never deny it. In fact, he would brag about his affairs and sometimes even go into detail. He once told Mother that he liked to have sex with women that were, "heavy in the front and big at the bottom," – unlike Mother, he'd say, "who was nothing but ugly bone and had no more good fucking left."

The standards to which we were held as children were beyond attainment. Yet, our parents achieved nothing.

I remember an evening when my mother was entertaining a man she had picked up in a local bar. I always knew when she was going to be bringing a man home. Mother would put on one of the few dresses that had not been shredded by Father's rage. She wore a lot of mascara, bright green or blue, and her lipstick was put on so thick it would flake in spots. Mother would somehow make her hair big and puffy like cotton and then coat it with so much hairspray that when she patted it you could hear crackling noises. Her dress was way too short, showing off the top of her nylons where they hooked to a garter belt. Completing the outfit would be a pair of either red or black high-heeled shoes, and when she bent over to buckle the straps, I saw she was not wearing panties.

She had instructed me to sneak into the bedroom and steal money from the man's wallet while they had audible cruel sex. Their grunts and groans were enough to turn my stomach, and the pressure from crawling along on my belly nearly caused me to vomit. I did as I was told and slid backward out of the bedroom. After finishing with my mother, the man dressed and discovered the money missing. My mother stood aside while he beat me, calling me a "nigger thief." She said and did nothing.

As we went back into the bedroom, Carter called out toward the closet. "Lynn! Lynn!" But there was no answer. I jumped every time he shouted. "We've got to go up there," he said.

It was more of a crawl space than a closet. The platform base was a couple of feet above the floor. Once inside the closet, Lynn could easily stand. Her head came within only four inches of the attic opening. Carter and I had to squat bent over upon entering the closet, but we could sit cross-legged comfortably inside the closet walls. Standing upright, we could also pop back the panel door and pull ourselves up and into the attic without any difficulty. With the use of a small three-rung stepladder, Lynn could easily do the same. When the stepladder was placed atop the platform of the crawlspace and she stood on its top step, she would be waist-high inside the attic. Then, all she would have to do is lift one knee up, place it on the attic floor, and crawl inside.

"Go up in the attic and look around," Carter said.

An image of my head being lopped off the moment it stuck through opening of the attic flashed across my brain and caused me to immediately reply, "No fucking way."

"You're a pussy!" Carter said. It was a lame attempt to force me into going, and he knew it.

The attic is going to kill me after all, I thought.

On the nights when Mother was using the bedroom I shared with Carter to *entertain*, I sometimes slept in this bedroom – Mother's room. It was also called the sewing room, because that is where she kept the old Singer sewing machine. The kind that had a metal push plate for your foot. I would watch Mother operate it sometimes, but that was when I was much younger and when she still sewed like normal mothers.

As I would lay there sucking in the dust from the dirty sheets, I would try not to hear the rattling and bumping of whatever lived in the attic. I believed the noises came from all the monsters who had found this house, with all its evil, a comfortable place to reside.

I would lie awake with all the memories of the things Mother did to me in the same bed. The same things she did with strangers.

I would lie awake and the dark would play tricks on me – like when I thought the old sewing dummy had been Mother hiding in the shadows. I could not breathe until I realized it was not her.

This room was filled with awful memories and a dark scary attic.

The thought of having to ascend into the attic, without even a flashlight, was too stressful to bear, and I began spiraling toward another episode. Carter must have noticed; therefore, he rendered me a swift but solid slap across the face. The room, although dark aside from the moonlight, flashed in many different colors. First a pure, dazzling white. This was most beautiful. Then it flashed a lovely green. Then it flashed red, and I, again, was completely aware of my surroundings.

"Don't trip out on me, Gregg. We have to go . . . We have to get up there now!" Carter was right, of course. It had been several minutes since we last heard anything, and for all we knew, Lynn was suffocating right above us.

I could hear my mother sanctimoniously bleating out the words, "Why didn't you boys help her?" The little voice in my head returned, *Why didn't you*? Ah, yes, there was wisdom in that voice, but I would have never allowed it to speak aloud – I mean, if you knew what was good for you, and I knew quite well. I learned all the wrinkles of the games the liars played. And knowing this did not make me happy. Wisdom, I had found out, never did.

We moved closer to the closet, and therefore toward the attic. Carter was standing close enough to rest one hand on the platform and the other on the cheap molding which framed the outside of the closet. I imagined something big and hairy reaching out of the darkness and grabbing his hand, pulling him inside the closet and up into the attic.

Then I saw something in the corner, and my heart sank. Just inside the closet, sitting directly beneath the attic, was the stepladder – the same one Lynn sometimes used when she wanted to reach something high above the kitchen counter. Now that we were right up on the closet, I could make out the three worn steps fastened with rusting metal tubes.

"She used the ladder to get up there. Oh, shit. She's up there," I muttered to myself, but Carter, standing so close, heard every word.

"No shit, Sherlock," he replied, another one of his famous truisms. He pulled the stepladder out of the closet, and set it inside the bedroom. We both climbed inside the closet at the same time, and in the narrow opening, our shoulders bumped. "Watch the bite, you freak!" Carter hissed. I could see the scarlet blood creeping through his shirt.

The attic was directly above us, and I could smell the aging wood and blown insulation. *That must be what hell smells like*, I thought.

Once inside the closet and crouching on the platform, I stood up too far and banged part of the attic panel with my head. I ducked so quickly it banged back down against its frame, but did not fall back into place.

"Go ahead and open it, Gregg! Hurry!" Carter said.

"Fuck no!" I said, and my voice was shaking badly.

The attic panel was now more askew, turning the former pie shape of an opening into a wedge. A puff of wind blew down on top of my head that felt like cold breath.

Carter whispered, "On three. I'll hit the attic panel and you stand up and look inside…Ready? One…two…"

"Wait!" I shrieked.

But it was too late. There was a loud bang as Carter punched the thin plywood panel of the attic door, and it flew off haphazardly. First hitting the rafters and then coming down hard and bouncing against the ceiling. It made a rattling sound and came to rest somewhere just above our heads. The damn thing sounded like it was going to come crashing right through the drywall of the ceiling.

The wind blew down from the attic and carried along with it a rancid smell. The air came in both warm and cold pockets. Unexpectedly, there came another bump, and it sounded close, followed by a very loud and familiar scream. I felt woozy, like I was going to pass out. As I began to slip further away, mercifully down to a soundless depth, I heard the scream again, and this time, I was positive it had come from Lynn.

CHAPTER SIX

CARTER STOOD WAVERINGLY, trying to hold me steady. Inside the attic, the screams grew louder. At first, they sounded far away, but were not far away at all. They were right above me. The unconsciousness I was fighting made them appear that way.

"Wake up, Gregg!" Carter shouted, and an eerie feeling slid around my brain.

"Poke your goddamn head up there!" he said.

This time, I did what Carter told me to do. I was too tired and weak to fight him any longer. I slowly stood up, and standing completely upright, my head cleared the opening to the attic, leveling off at the top of my shoulders. My head was now completely exposed, and I braced myself for the decapitation that most assuredly would come from behind.

"What do you see?" Carter asked, and I could hear the anxiety in his voice. I could feel his chest heaving in and out against my side.

"Nothing," I replied and secretly thanked God. Inside the attic, there were long wooden joists, which stank of rot.

There were other objects strewn about, but I couldn't make them out. To be honest, I didn't want to know. My eyes adjusted, and I saw one of the objects against the far wall directly in front of me. It was an old highchair, and it looked as if whoever placed it up there had simply tossed it against the wall. One of its legs were busted and left dangling by a piece of thin wood. A vent was cut out to allow the attic to cool, and I noticed this was how the air was blowing in from outside. I was admiring the round hole, which looked like a ship's portal, when a gust of wind that felt like more cold breath blew against my face, making me scream.

"What the fuck?" Carter yelled.

"Nothing! The wind scared me."

"Well, is Lynn up there or not? Christ! We heard her scream!"

Before I could answer, the broken leg of the highchair caught a bit of wind and banged against the attic wall. I screamed again, and when I did, I dropped so fast it felt like the earth dropped out from underneath me. One of my legs kicked Carter, knocking him off balance. He fell, his body pushing mine forward, causing me to smack my face on the side of the closet wall. Had he not reached out and braced himself, I would have absorbed the full impact of both our bodies.

There was the familiar taste of blood almost instantly. I figured I had swallowed enough of it over the years to equal what my heart pumped throughout my entire body. We both continued to fall, crashing downward, and ended up splayed like pixie-sticks atop the platform of the closet. Legs and arms were so tangled it was difficult to tell where Carter's appendages ended and mine began.

"For fuck's sake, Gregg!" Carter shouted.

I wanted to leave and give up entirely. I looked toward the bedroom and thought that if I were to push hard enough off the wall behind me, I could clear Carter and leap from the closet. It was an inviting prospect. I would run away and this time for good.

We were both gasping and covered in sweat. My upper-lip stung and had a sandpaper texture to it. It felt swollen already and threatening to burst. Somewhere nearby, a motorcycle blatted. "Hogs," we called them and they were everywhere.

"Mom!" I blurted. "Mom will be home soon!"

Carter saw the fear in my eyes and scrambled away, untangling us both, stood up, and pulled me to my feet. We were moving again, and soon I was standing upright inside the attic opening. The thought of my head being lopped off was now a dull fret.

"Lynn! Lynn!" I cried. Nothing. Not a sound.

I turned around, doing a full 360. My eyes adjusted, and something in the corner of the attic moved. It moved and wept. "Lynn?" I said cautiously. It was Lynn all right, and she was huddled into a ball and squished into a corner.

With as much urgency as I could muster, but still sound calm, I called to her. "Lynn, come over here!"

She did not reply and only sat motionless.

Carter yelled, "Lynn! Get down! Mom and Dad will be here soon!"

Upon hearing Carter's last words, Lynn began to cry out loud. "Dad's going to kill me! Mom said Dad's going to rape me and kill me!"

She kept repeating these words, and it made me cold inside. Our father would have never hurt Lynn, and perhaps this is what made Mother angry. Before my parents left, Mother must have made sure to leave Lynn absolutely convinced Dad would hurt her in every way possible.

Mother never beat Lynn; instead, she used a form of mental torture that left Lynn frozen and shattered – an emotional anguish that would draw from her a profound and soundless weeping.

Mother often warned Lynn that she was going to be raped by one of the neighborhood boys while she slept in her bed. She would describe in great detail how the twin boys down the block would take turns. It was easy to believe Mother, because the identical brothers that we liked to call *the twins,* had already been arrested. It could have been for burglary for all we knew, but it was enough to make Mother's stories believable. They were so believable that Lynn lived in constant fear and stopped leaving her bedroom window open at night during the summer, regardless of how hot it was – even when the heat became so stifling it seemed to suck all the air out of her room.

If it was not the horrific stories of rape and molestation Mother was force-feeding Lynn, it was the brutal destruction of her dolls that Lynn was subjected to. Mother would take what few dolls Lynn had and tear them apart, leaving pieces of them all over her bedroom. There would be a mass of arms and legs scattered all over Lynn's room, miniature pink limbs snapped off, broken and twisted torsos strewn in many directions. Her playthings ruined.

Lynn would kick the portions of worthless plastic into her closet and shut the door. She then lay atop her bed, crying so hard that she would eventually fall over on her side with her hands between her thin little girl's legs and fall fast asleep.

"Lynn, what did Mom tell you?" I asked, each word coming out more gently than the last.

In long harsh shaking breaths, she said, "Dad was going to pull my underwear down and put his thing in me until it bled, and cover my mouth so I couldn't breathe."

I could both hear and see Mother telling Lynn this. Her words would have a tone like honey, but would hang in the air, heavy with manipulation. To Lynn, Mother's words must have sounded like a hideous promise based on an absolute truth.

Father would never harm Lynn. He never even harmed Carter and me, and we were both boys and older than Lynn.

He abandoned all of us, that was certain. However, he never hit us like he hit Mother. During the worst of a beating he was giving Mother, when Father punched her and the walls until his knuckles bled, even then he would only push us out of the way. In my mind, it just wasn't possible for Father to harm Lynn. Perhaps also because it was one of the few remaining strands of fabric that held what was left of my sanity together.

Carter broke the silence after Lynn spoke. I had not known what to say and could only stare at the top of Lynn's head, while she pulled up her knees closer to her chin.

"Lynn! Mom is lying to you! Now crawl over to Gregg, and get down!" Carter shrieked.

She unlatched her arms from around her legs and began moving in my direction. When she assumed a crawling position, something dropped from her sweater and thumped against the rafters. There was a sudden yellowish burst of light, and then it was extinguished.

A flashlight, I thought. Then it occurred to me that this was the eye. As she continued to move closer, I could see Lynn was trying to hold back deep sobs. Her hair hung down and dragged along, catching little pieces of insulation. Lynn muttered she was freezing, but it came out "fweezing," because she could not pronounce her R's. When our hands touched in order to help lower her down, I felt how cold she was.

"Turn around, Lynn, and back towards me," I said, so I could better curl my arms around her waist. Carter and I worked in tandem to lower Lynn down. When she was completely on the platform of the closet, Carter jumped down and then me. I turned, grabbed Lynn, and swung her down and onto the bedroom floor.

"Damn, you're heavy," I said, but smiling. Elated that Lynn was safe, the three of us got out of the bedroom as fast as we could and away from the closet.

"We'll wait in the living room," Carter said.

When we left the bedroom, Lynn was still clinging to my shirt.

"Yur bleeden," she said to Carter.

"Yeah. Ask num-nuts about that."

This got us laughing. Even so, I saw there were still tears in Lynn's eyes, and when she looked up at me, I saw they were pleading and swollen.

The three of us took our places in the living room and waited in agony for Mother and Father to return.

Carter sat in a chair, while Lynn and I sat on opposite ends of the couch. We wanted to sit next to one another, but if our mother caught us too close, we would get in trouble for being too sexual. From the vantage of the couch, I could see enough of the driveway through the filthy curtains to offer up a warning when Dad's Thunderbird pulled up. As if Lynn was reading my thoughts, she made a low whimpering sound. There was a thick feeling of anxiety in the air. Carter would offer up a reminder, every now and then, that we couldn't tell Mother about the attic incident. I looked outside again and saw a bag floating in the wind and lightly skipping down the empty street. It looked like a Holsum Bread bag, and it reminded me of when I ran from the corner store with the large rack full of bread. The driver nearly caught me that day and if he had, he would have really done a number on me. I looked up just then and saw a flash of red outside the window.

I was daydreaming again and forgot to warn Carter and Lynn, which caused them to jump and scream when the front door came crashing inward. Father's eyes were blazing with anger, and with one hand, he held up our mother by a strap of her bra and what was left of her dress. "Here's your whore of a mother!" he bellowed. We sat frozen. Mother's bright red lipstick looked smeared, but then I saw it was blood that covered her whole mouth and lower jaw. There were thick red lines between her false teeth, which were noticeably cracked – most likely from a solid punch.

Instead of just leaving her at the bar, Father had brought her home to show her children proof that she was exactly everything he claimed her to be - a whore. He rushed into the house, dragging Mother like a marionette with its strings cut – holding her up with his massive fist.

"Your fucking Mother tried to screw every drunk in the bar!" our father explained, as if to justify the beating he gave her. Although none of us doubted he was exaggerating.

Mother just stood there, as if in a daze, looking like a rag doll. Father finally released his grip and gave Mother a good shove. She went sprawling forward and fell to the floor.

I was by her side immediately, and then Father's meaty hand grabbed my arm and flung me backward. "Don't help that cunt!" he commanded.

Inside the shoe closet, just off the front door, was a long broomstick. The brush was lost, but it served as a disciplinary tool Mother used on us quite often. Carter ran for it and snatched it in his hands. He stood defiantly in front of Father and was dwarfed by the size difference.

"Swing that, boy, and I'll knock you on your ass!" Father said and then slapped the stick from Carter's hands. It bounced on the carpet and then rolled to rest underneath the couch. We had no phone to call the police. The neighbors didn't want to get involved and didn't care. We were helpless to do anything but watch in horror. Mother staggered to her feet, and Father lunged for her.

Father swung with precision force, crushing the left side of Mother's face with one blow. I got a glimpse of her eye just as it popped from its socket. Her limp body slammed against a huge mirror mural fastened to the wall, leaving an outline of her head. The impact of Mother's skull shattered what was once a beautiful black and white rendition of the Zumbrota Covered Bridge. She then fell to the floor in a slump and did not move. The eye dangled, and I wondered if she could see her cheek.

Father stood over her and continued to swing as if she were still standing. It wasn't until he caught his reflection in the broken mirror that he stopped. He looked puzzled at the face staring back at him, as if he were looking at a total stranger. "Help your mother, Gregg!" Father bellowed, but never looked at me.

He turned to leave, and Carter attempted to tackle him, but bounced off as if he just ran into a brick wall. Father pushed past Carter and simply walked out the door, saying nothing and lighting a cigarette as he left. Moments later, after he eased the car out of the driveway, all that was left of him was a trail of smoke that still hung in the air near the door. That and Mother, who lay dying at the feet of her three children.

Carter ran from the house and down the street to the only pay phone for at least five miles. He knew just to press "0" for help. We had all learned that from past emergencies. Lynn and I waited with Mother. She lay still on the living room floor. Her face was blank and smooth, as if sleeping with her eyes open, but now only one socket was inhabited.

Carter returned from making the call minutes later. Shortly thereafter, the police arrived with their bubblegum lights flashing. They pulled into the driveway and kept their lights flashing the whole time. When they entered the house, they found me kneeling next to Mother, shaking her arm, and begging her not to die. Lynn knelt by Mother's feet, rubbing her legs. Carter stood by the door and looked on as tears streamed down his pudgy cheeks. The three of us begged the police to save Mother. The abused now prayed for the abuser. She was cruel, but she was also our mother.

The paramedics came soon after the police had arrived, followed by a social worker. The police and the paramedics looked like they knew exactly what to do.

One officer wrote things down while appearing to take information from a paramedic working on Mother. Another spoke on a radio that would occasionally squawk loudly, making me jump.

Time had taken an ungainly hop forward.

The paramedic's voice was flat and mechanic, "Fractures: jaw, skull, nose, lacerated *something*, disconnected *something*, ... eye." "Vitals: BP, pulse ... *something*, swollen ... *something*, approximate age, weight, height ... *something*, gender: female, alcohol ... *something*."

I remember the sense of being in the way and pulled. My left hand was removed from where it was underneath Mother's head by the paramedic. It came away warm with blood soaking my palm. I begged for them to save her, and with every breath between deep guttural sobs, I begged some more.

I do not remember seeing the social worker come in, but I remember her trying to pull me away from Mother. She gently tried to coax me away at first, but when that did not work, she tried more forcefully. Then she would look at Mother's face all busted up and lose interest for a little bit, then sort of snap back, and try to pull me away again.

Between the officers and the paramedics, there must have been a half-dozen people working on my mother. I was not making it easy because I kept screaming for her to breathe and kept yanking on her torn dress. No matter how many times the social worker told me to do so, I would not let go.

With the help of an officer, the social worker finally got me into the kitchen, by mostly pulling and half carrying me. Carter and Lynn were already in there, but I do not remember them going into the kitchen. I do remember not caring about what the social worker had to say; even though she cared enough to get us some water from the sink and kneel down to talk. It was probably something about how Mother was going to be okay, but I did not care about that either. All I knew was that I needed to be in the next room. Next to Mother. The social worker held me while I struggled to get free. Finally, breaking her grip, I ran back into the living room. The thing that used to be Mother was laying with her back flat against the floor, and her arms and legs up close next to her body like she were at attention. The top of her dress was ripped open and her bra was askew, showing too much of her breasts. I remember wanting to cover her with a blanket.

This time, one of the police officers caught me before reaching Mother and lifted me up, pulling me in the opposite direction in which she lay. I remember kicking and squirming to get away and back to Mother. He just kept telling me that it was going to be okay, but he was lying. I knew it. I fought even harder. I fought with all the strength I had left. Carter and Lynn held one another and cried, yelling at me to stop. Not until I saw her whole body jump up from the floor, like something pushed her hard from underneath, did I stop. I stopped dead cold.

The social worker was still there somewhere, but did not bother with me anymore. The police officer that pulled me away had his arm wrapped around my chest, but my feet were now firmly on the floor. When Mother jumped again, I felt the vibration running up my legs. All of a sudden, it was quiet, and right before she jumped a third time, a paramedic in a white and red shirt kneeling almost on top of her yelled something. It sounded like "Clear."

Mother bounced upward and then came crashing to the floor. A paramedic had wrapped her head in gauze, which covered the socket once void of its eye. The gauze was thicker over that socket, and I remember wondering if the eye was popped back inside its hole. Mother's other eye, the one that was intact, was swollen shut. The upper and lower skin swelled to the point they pressed against one another over where her eye used to be. *She's blind,* I thought.

Her face, normally skeletal, was puffy and plump beneath the gauze of the head wrapping. I could see the blood-soaked roots of her hair turning the white gauze a brilliant red, which had already formed a visible stain on the carpet.

The paramedic pushed on her chest and squeezed air into her mouth with this plastic bag. I knew it was just a matter of time before I would hear this audible crack and his hands would go right through her tiny breast. I watched and waited. But I didn't pray. My head was scrambled, and I could not concentrate long enough to pray. Prayer would come later, as it always did, but for now there was no use in that.

Across the street and peering through her living room curtains was Mrs. Jacobson. The lights and commotion must have woken her up. She had Jessica's phone number from years back and must have called her. The neighbors had gotten used to seeing the police at our house, but not an ambulance. Mrs. Jacobson must have known it was serious. I bet she figured Father finally killed Mother or Mother finally killed one or all of her children.

When they were rolling Mother out on the gurney, Jessica was running into the house. "Get in the car!" she said.

The adrenaline was making me sick, and I vomited twice in the yard before climbing into the backseat of Jessica's car. The dome light was too sharp on my eyes, and I wanted to close them, but was afraid I'd miss Mother waving to me before they closed the two heavy metal doors of the ambulance. She never moved.

Jessica would not drive us to the hospital. I gave the ambulance one more look as we drove away in the opposite direction. Its siren blaring and probably waking up the entire neighborhood. I was both ashamed and afraid.

The street curved around an old dark house I remembered well. I would pass the house each time before the field opened itself up. I never saw anyone around the house. It was always dark. I began to weep.

Raising my head every now and then to look out the window, I saw we were driving past a cornfield. *A good hiding place*, I thought to myself. I did not remember any cornfields near our house. Where we lived was a perfect blend of both suburban white trash and inner city deterioration. However, this was different. It was all green and full of color. Clean. That's what stuck in my mind the most. Everything was so clean.

From the backseat, I asked Jessica where we were going. "My house," she said, then went back to driving. Carter and Lynn sat quietly.

I continued staring out the window at the night lit up by the street lights and watched the lines of the road get real close to the car, then slide away. When we would drive under a bridge, it would get dark and cast a quick reflection of my face in the window. I looked tired.

Obsessed with spitting, it was bothering me something awful not to be able to roll down the window and chuck the glob of saliva building up in my mouth. It was my new compulsion. However, I figured if I spat, Jessica would get mad and maybe even pull the car over to smack me. So I forced the warm goop down my throat and had to fight back the urge to throw up.

As we drove, Jessica suddenly spoke. Her tone was matter of fact. "You know he raped me?"

I thought of what Mother told Lynn before she went out drinking with Dad. I thought about this for a long time and wondered if it were true. I grew increasingly anxious thinking that maybe Mother was right about Dad. Maybe he was going to rape Lynn.

When we reached Jessica's house, all I wanted was sleep. Jessica let me lay down in one of the bedrooms, and I was asleep instantly. I did not awake until late afternoon the following day.

Upon waking, I was disoriented and had forgotten where I was. I climbed down off the bed and went from room to room looking for Mother. The house was empty. I was terribly frightened and called her name, but no one answered. I went back to the bed in which I had first slept and laid down again. Moments later it came back to me what had happened and where I was.

The curtains were drawn making the room dark. Perhaps Jessica had taken Carter and Lynn out for a walk. While laying on the bed much too large for me, the panic began to rise up. I tried to focus on the cornfield, but I kept going back to Mother and wondered if she were alive. A very small part of me found some relief in the fact she might have died. Feeling ashamed, the tears rolled down my cheeks, creating a small harbor upon my pillow. However, shame soon turned to fear when I thought I had caught a glimpse of something black standing at the edge of my bed.

Both very afraid and hungry, I slowly moved under the blankets trying not to look at whatever stood in the shadows at the end of the bed. I drew my knees up, all the way to my chest, and curled into a tight little ball. After pulling the covers over my head and squishing my eyes shut, I eventually fell back to sleep. In the empty dark room, I slept restlessly.

CHAPTER SEVEN

I MUST HAVE SLEPT for an hour or more, when a sudden clatter shook me awake. I was glad for it too, because it brought me out of a terrible dream I was having. All I remember about the dream was that it had to do with Mother and very unpleasant things.

For several minutes, I just lay in the bed and gradually noticed that I was soaked in sweat. When I threw the covers off me, I noticed that I had urinated as well. I was filled immediately with sharp fear that Jessica would get upset for what I had done. Now very still, I continued to lay there. Several minutes passed, and with my eyes open while breathlessly listening, I heard voices. There was movement outside my door.

Unexpectedly, I began to panic and started heaving in-and-out, as if I was drowning. I could not breathe, and my windpipe closed off altogether. The worse it became, the more I fought the feeling I was being strangled. The room disappeared, and there was blackness all around me.

I felt the mattress beneath me and lurched forward. Vomit now covered the large wet pool of urine. Swinging my legs over the side of the bed, the last of the vomit spurted out of my mouth and onto the floor.

I sat on the edge of the bed for several minutes, taking in air and trying to control my breathing. The anxiety slowly subsided and my vision came back. When my breathing returned to normal, I knelt down and used my shirt, tossed on the floor earlier, to mop up the puke. It gagged me, but I fought the urge to throw up again.

Gathering up my nerve, I walked out of the bedroom and followed the voices into the kitchen. In one hand was the crumpled up vomit-soaked shirt.

Jessica took one look at the flakes of puke stuck to my belly and sighed. Whatever scolding she was prepared to launch was short-lived the moment I burst into tears. After a quick rinse, Jessica then gave me one of her shirts to wear, which hung down on me like a small dress. She brought me into the kitchen where Carter and Lynn were, and fed all of us. We were starving and swallowed our food without chewing. After we'd eaten, Jessica laid me back down in another bedroom. Naked underneath while my soiled clothes were washed, I was clean and my stomach full. I eagerly crawled underneath the covers. In doing so, I was asleep in only minutes. This time, I did not dream.

When Carter woke me, it was nearing dusk. He told me the hospital had called and Mother was going to be okay. I crawled out of bed and noticed with great relief I had not peed myself. Carter's face looked tired, like the Mitchell boy who lived down the street when he came back from Vietnam. The same boy whose father had shot himself in the head when his son was off to war.

My clothes, washed and dried, were laid out on the chair in the bedroom. I dressed and walked into the hallway. I saw Jessica carrying a bucket under her arm and away from the bedroom where I had gotten sick. She then disappeared into the kitchen, seeing me but not saying a word. A look of disgust hung on her face. Embarrassed, I looked down. It was midsummer and when I passed the room Jessica had just left, it smelled of cooked vomit.

We would come to find out while Mother was in the hospital that she had refused to press charges against Father. We were not surprised. It wasn't the first time.

Two weeks passed before Mother was released from the hospital. The surgery to fit her eye back into its socket left her with a patch for the next two months. Father had also fractured her skull and broken her jawbone. Mother would be left with a permanent sag to one side of her mouth. When I heard this, I thought of the children's rhyme: "There was a crooked man that wore a crooked smile." Jessica had laughed sarcastically when she made the remark that Mother's mouth would be latched together, so she'd have to drink her wine through a straw until she was healed.

The two weeks we spent at Jessica's were much better than being with Mother. There weren't any beatings or molestations. We ate regular meals and our basic needs were met. However, Jessica did not want us there, and I could tell.

I realized even if we had asked to live with Jessica, she would have said no. Ordinary children would have been a handful, and we were not ordinary children. Living with the experiences of Mother's madness and Father's neglect, Jessica could see it had left us with many issues. Maybe she did not want to be reminded of what she left behind years before.

Jessica was married, but near divorce due to her husband's infidelity – and hers. She had two children of her own from two different fathers. Her home was already in turmoil, and we would only add more problems. I now knew for sure that our only hope of ever getting away from Mother was with Lauren.

It had been Jessica who first put the idea in our heads that Lauren was a possibility. Occasionally, Jessica would stop by the house, and she happened to come by once after Mother had just beaten me. Pinning Mother against the wall, Jessica had threatened to take us kids away. Soon afterwards, we had overheard that Jessica had called Lauren, and they discussed our options. It was the first breath of hope I had in a long time.

I hadn't seen Lauren in a few years. I had been only three when she married and left. Carter had only been five and actually attended her wedding. It was there he drank the alcohol punch and fell down the cement stairs of the church, rendering him a nice gash across one eyebrow needing stitches.

It had been a few years since Lauren had visited us last, and then it had only been briefly. However, I felt this aspect would prove valuable. Perhaps she would not remember us that well. There would be no preconceived notions, no prejudices, leaving the possibility of wanting to help her half brothers and sister. If she really knew us, there would be no way she'd ever take us in. We were damaged goods.

The two weeks with Jessica were over far too soon and she said that we needed to go with her to pick up Mother from the hospital. Upon hearing this, fear struck my heart, and I ran and hid outside. From beyond the screen of bushes that lined Jessica's driveway, I squatted and peered through the tiny branches, watching Carter and Lynn climb into her car. Jessica was already behind the driver's seat, and everyone was waiting on me. Her husband would stay with the kids. I knew there was no choice but to go. So I stood and rounded the brush, then slowly walked to the car and entered the opened door. Not saying anything, I slid in next to Carter and shut the door behind me with a bang, which made Lynn jump and Carter a little bit too.

My eyes welled up before the car left the driveway, and the world swayed and waved. I leaned forward and laid my head on the back of the front seat. "Don't get sick in this car," Jessica said. I fought back the growth of puke that wanted to come up and kept swallowing the thickening spit. By the time we were at the hospital, the nausea had passed, but not the fear of seeing Mother.

A nurse wheeled Mother into the waiting room of the lobby, and I did not recognize her at first. She was dressed in a mint-green pajama set with matching slippers. Her head was wrapped with fresh gauze, and she wore a patch over the damaged eye. The one that had been popped clean out of its socket. The swelling had completely subsided from the other eye, but a blue-black circle now enveloped it. Her lips were still a little swollen and turned out a bit. The gown exposed a large area of her breast, which was clearly marked with an ugly scarlet and yellowing patch. There was sure to be another one just like it circling and just beneath her ribcage. The paddles had left their telltale sign of rendering Mother enough electricity to jump-start her heart.

I stood just a few inches away from the wheelchair. There was an awkward pause, and then I went to hug her. She pushed me away.

Baring temporary dentures, Mother barked, "Watch my head!" while moving only her lips and straining to speak through a jaw wired shut.

Her breath was harsh and rapid, and she glared at me, as if this had all been my fault. Mother continued to look at me. Through me. Her hands were clasped in her lap. I could see the ugly bruising from the needles that left black and yellowing streaks running up her arms, looping around, and disappearing behind her gaunt biceps. The veins protruded from the crotch of her forearms leaving lumpy blue lines of what looked like toothpaste under skin. Somehow, Mother blamed me for what had happened, and I knew when the wounds healed and she had regained her strength, things would go back to the way they were.

The five of us drove home in silence. Jessica helped Mother into the house and onto the couch. Mother looked at the wall mural and seeing the break in the mirror quickly looked away. Jessica left the house soon after Mother was settled. Neither of them saying a word. I walked outside with Jessica and gave her a hug goodbye. She told me to be careful and then left. With the fumes from Jessica's car exhaust still lingering in the dank humid air, I walked back inside the house to begin caring for Mother.

Weeks passed, and I fell into the usual rhythm of catering to Mother's needs. It was somewhat different. Perhaps even a little better. She was too weak to beat me, and therefore most of my days were filled with running errands to purchase her wine. Even better was the fact she had none of the interest in the sex either. I would help change her dressings, and early on when I had pulled away the gauze I saw bloody bits of tissue clinging to it.

Jessica had been right about Mother sipping wine through a straw. "Help me!" Mother would hiss through her fastened-together jaw, and I would bring the straw to her mouth, due to hands far too unsteady to do it herself. I purchased, poured, and helped Mother drink her wine. I got her blankets, propped her pillows, and made her a nice bed on the couch. Mother was not thankful, nor was she nicer during this time, just more feeble, and I knew her strength would one day return.

The day it did was when Jessica came back over; she took Mother to get her stitches removed from her head and the wire removed from her jaw. While Jessica and Mother were out, I took the well-deserved opportunity to play outside. I spent time under the apple tree where it was cool and silent, and I was blessedly alone. It was from under the apple tree I heard Jessica pull into the driveway, and I immediately went to greet her and Mother. By the time I rounded the backyard and passed through the gate, Jessica was already pulling away. I waved and she honked a return.

It felt like there was a hot stone in the pit of my stomach as I walked toward the front door. Something felt very wrong. As soon as I walked inside and pulled the screen door closed, Mother hit the back of my head with something heavier than her hand, and I saw a quick flash of light. I stumbled forward, and my knees buckled. My first thought was, *She must have been hiding behind the front door.*

As I knelt away from her, she followed up with another bash to the back of my head. Something broke apart, sending colorful pieces everywhere. She had used her favorite ashtray – a bored out seashell I always thought had been much too beautiful to put out her cigarettes. Its many broken pieces told me that I would no longer need to fret about that.

"Get me a goddamn cigarette!" Mother demanded. It had been nearly two months since she had last smoked. Father had seen to that by his gift to her in the form of a jaw securely wired shut. Still on my knees, delirious from the hit to the back of my head, I frantically swept my hands around the living room floor looking for her cigarettes.

"I'll show you the works! I'll show you what it feels like!" Mother shouted.

From the gash Mother had opened on the back of my head, I felt warm fresh blood beginning to trickle down my back, following my spine, which then proceeded to blaze a trail down the inside of my pants and into the crack of my butt.

Unmoving and still in a kneeling position, waiting for the dizziness to pass, I tried going into a fantasy. Thinking through the pain was a mechanism I developed. Throughout the abuse, I would concentrate on an object around the room. It was a skill I perfected and had many opportunities to do so. It was always at the ready in my mind. Somewhere hidden and secret, yet nearby.

The blood running down my spine tickled and sent electric waves all over my body. I stayed focused on an object and continued to follow a speck of light, trundling down an endless tunnel. For the most part, it was quiet, broken occasionally by Mother telling me to stay put and not move. I remained staring at the carpet and let the nausea pass. My head was a thumping beat of pain. Although my back was to her I could hear and smell Mother smoking. She had found her cigarettes.

My legs were going numb from kneeling and there was a relentless buzzing echo inside my ears. A thumping clamor coordinated with my heartbeat, followed by a feeling of a thousand razor blades being jammed into my head. Just then Carter came home and, upon seeing me, he shouted, "All he wanted to do was come out and play!"

Carter helped me to my feet and to the bathroom. We passed Mother on the couch and she took a moment to look at us, at me anyway, and then went back to absently smoking her cigarette.

With an old plastic cup, Carter leaned me over the tub and rinsed the back of my head. Thankfully, the cut wasn't as bad as we initially thought. Carter dabbed the cut with toilet paper and poured Peroxide over it, making my head hurt worse. Every time he dumped Peroxide into the cut, it felt as though razor blades filling my head were going to slice through my temples and rip my skull clean apart.

Exhausted, I went to our bedroom and lay down. Carter lay down with me, but before doing so, he got me a blanket from the floor. It was piss-smelling but comforting.

The pain in my head reminded me of when one of my molars had rotted. The decay had eaten most of the tooth, forming a jagged point that kept stabbing me in the cheek. I remember one of my older sisters taking me to the free-clinic and having the tooth removed. The dentist held up the tooth after yanking it from its sick socket and showed it to me. I then received a stern lecture on proper dental hygiene. A lecture meant not for me, but for children who actually owned toothbrushes.

My siblings and I had always been survivors. For example, we learned early that our immediate survival depended upon knowing basic first aid. In time, it seemed only natural to always know where to find a bottle of alcohol, peroxide, gauze, ointments, and rags. Most of this stuff was left over from the time my older sisters lived with us. The house never underwent a thorough cleaning so nothing was ever thrown out. Regardless, we stole food when desperate and a bottle of peroxide was not out of the question.

Rags were always easy to come by. They came from our sheets, pillowcases, and underclothes. We wore them. A shirt quickly became makeshift wrapping for a cut. Anything to stop the bleeding. We learned any cut left without proper attention would fester, because they often did. Knowing this was not the sign of great insight or intelligence. Even an animal will lick its wounds. It was purely instinctive.

Feeling safe next to Carter, I began to drift off to sleep. The pain in my head was going away as long as I did not move it. I thought of a cat I once had – my cat, Sambirdio. Thinking of him always helped me fall asleep. More than a pet, he was my miracle. A gray tiger cat I chose from a litter of nine being given away by a neighbor girl. He had emerald green eyes with gold flecks and a small mouth that always looked like it was smiling. Downy fur, which was soft as cotton, covered his body. Long sharp claws that never scratched me and a mewing that sounded like a musical mumble. I will never understand why Sam made me feel braver; all I know is that he did.

Shutting my eyes and determined to give sleep every chance, I kept thinking of how Sam had recently died. For two years, Sam was my cat and the best friend I ever had. I would think of him often, and weep now almost automatically. At night, I would listen for his motor purr next to my ear on my filthy pillow. He had suffered for several months, but his death still felt unexpected.

Remembering how I came home to find him gone started the razor blades in my head again. As I thought more about how he died, something rose in my throat and almost choked me.

PART TWO
The Struggle for Life

"Hope is the thing with feathers
That perches in the soul.
And sings the tune
Without the words,
And never stops at all."

Emily Dickinson

CHAPTER EIGHT

THE FIRST NIGHT WITH MY NEW KITTEN — the first night in what was to become an endless succession of falling in love, for the first time, with something that would love me in return — I made a promise to myself that I would not let him die.

All day I had kept the kitten concealed. The time would come when Mother found out, but the kitten was far too young, and I was far too lonely to care. She had no idea I had talked a neighbor girl into letting me take the runt of her cat's new litter. While I was over visiting the girl, I peeked into the litter and saw a hairless lump that had been cast off from its mother and lay shivering. Its pink mouth made little suckling motions.

While I sat watching all the other newborn kittens greedily suck at their mother's tits, I became increasingly upset. This kitten would die if I did not do something. I stuck the kitten in my front pocket and adjusted my clothes so it did not bulge out. Carefully taking the kitten home with me, I quickly ducked inside the house and found Carter and Lynn. With their help, we turned an old shoebox into a makeshift bed, laced with tissue paper, old news-papers, and torn fabric from clothes that should have been thrown out long ago. The kitten's new home was complete. Carter and Lynn would not tell Mother. We lied for each other all the time. It was a buddy system based on survival.

Inside the shoebox, the tiny kitten was buried in shreds of toilet paper, and the paper, wrapped around his tiny head, exposed only purple, puffy eyes and a small, pink mouth. He looked like a strange flower.

With an eyedropper borrowed from the neighbor girl and a few easy instructions from her as to how the kitten should be fed, I gently held the tip of the dropper against his tiny mouth and squeezed out one drop of instant milk. The drop of milk traced along the slit of his mouth, but the mouth did not open. I tried again, and this time I pushed the tip of the eyedropper a little harder, forcing the undersized opening apart just enough to get at least one drop of milk down his puny throat.

It worked! The kitten took to the eyedropper as if it was his mother's titty and drank about a quarter of the milk down in only a few minutes. I was elated to have something to care for that would love me back.

Hiding away in the closet below the attic was where I cared for the kitten. Perhaps it was this newfound responsibility, but I was no longer afraid of the attic. A few days later, his eyes opened and it was then I named him *Sam*. Later, I would add "*birdio*" at the end of his name after watching him chase birds in the backyard.

I spent a full summer tending to Sam, and it was wonderful. I recall being there when Sam grew a brownish-gray whisper of downy hair over his little body. I was there when he opened his eyes for the first time and looked up at me. I was there when Sam began to walk, at first with great difficulty and then later when he strode with the agility of a lion. I was there when Sam drank all by himself from a saucer and didn't need the eyedropper anymore.

Sam grew to be both playful and loving. I was happiest when strolling down the street with him darting in and out between my legs, falling behind and catching up again – or through the backyard, while Sam explored the edges of the fence, with the wind blowing in the summer and snow falling in winter.

Of course, Mother hated Sam. She would often chase him from whatever room he was in by pretending to lunge at him with snaring false teeth nearly jutting from her once-broken jaw. "I ought to kill that cat," she would say while sitting back down and lighting up another cigarette. I was careful to keep Sam from Mother, and Sam seemed careful to avoid her.

As often as we could, we would sit under the apple tree together. Sam would be on my lap while I combed his soft fur with my fingers. We would sit a long while, taking in the peacefulness. His breathing would slow and his motor would trail off to a low rumble as he gently fell asleep. I stole lunchmeat and cheese from the corner store to feed him. I also stole cans of cat food, bread, milk — and the always-popular fruit pie, which was for me.

Like me, Sam loved the smell of the lilac bush near the back of the yard. With him nestled in my arms like a baby, I would lean into the bush taking in deep breaths of lilac. My face would hover just above one of the pudgy groupings of bright pink flowers, sucking in the fragrant air. Sometimes, I'd glance down to see Sam doing the same thing.

Even though Sam possessed long, sharp claws that had never been trimmed, he would not scratch me – not even when I buried my face in his belly and made mumbling sounds. The soft pads of his paws would paddle my cheeks, but never did his claws come out.

As time passed with Sam, something stirred inside me. A feeling that I could not define filled me with a vengeance. The feeling grew stronger as I became older. It also seemed to be hidden until Sam woke it up somehow. When the feeling got to be too much and the tears stung at my eyes, I could reach down and take one of Sam's paws between my thumb and forefinger, giving it a gentle squeeze. This seemed to help, and he would always stare up at me with his usual quiet dignity.

Sam was everything to me. I could, and often would, weep while holding him. Allowing the tears to roll down my cheeks and disappear into his soft coat. I came to see Sam as another refuge. I was never too smelly or dirty for Sam. I was always welcomed and good enough. I was there for him, and he for me.

About a year had passed since I had first brought Sam home. My overall environment had not changed. As a matter of fact, it had become worse. Still, I did have SamBirdio. The more difficult my life became, the more I clung to my companionship with Sam. I couldn't imagine my life without him and rarely gave this terrible possibility much thought.

It was summertime again, and Sam and I took full advantage of it, spending as much time as we could outside. Sam had been sleeping soundly on my lap when Mother came crashing through the back door of the house and staggered toward the apple tree. There was a faint twitch from Sam, but he did not wake up. I found this to be very strange, even worrisome, but I did not have the luxury of giving the thought too much attention at the time.

Mother stopped short, and for a moment, it appeared that she forgot why she was outside. Then, as if in slow motion, I watched her begin moving again with more purpose than before. Carter now stood at the back door and was watching her. Lynn was playing up the street, and I could hear her calling to Alexis, Kyle's youngest sister.

Mother seemed to advance toward me in a slow plodding motion, and the nearer she drew, the darker her face became. She then reached in and dragged me from the apple tree. When she did, Sam awoke, hissed and ran away. Now she was above me, looming and hanging suspended. Her breathing was shallow and her eyes glared hypnotically. So close, I watched as they lost their color and drowsily merged, blending into hatred. Then I felt the first sting of her nails buried deep within the soft flesh under my chin.

She pulled me toward the back door. It felt as though my feet never touched the ground. As we crossed over the threshold, Carter reached for me and Mother stopped him short with one smooth slap to the face. He reeled backward, holding his cheek. Whatever courage he may have had before then was now gone.

Mother hauled me through the kitchen and into the living room then stopped. Grabbing my throat, which now felt hard and choky, she demanded to know what I did with her cigarettes. I could hardly breathe nor speak. "Where are my cigarettes?" Mother screamed.

Carter wept in the corner of the living room. Lynn had come in from playing, and I saw her now crouched next to him. Mother had most likely smoked the cigarettes or lost them. Her children spent many sleepless nights after the corner store was closed for the evening searching the house for her cigarettes.

I did not answer Mother at first; however, she was excellent at getting things out of me that not only I did not want to tell her, but that were entirely untrue. Therefore, I told Mother what she wanted to hear. "I took them," I said. "I smoked them with Kyle."

There was no reason to get Carter in trouble along with me. As soon as the lie left my mouth, her fist came crashing into it. My bottom lip exploded, shooting a spray of blood down the front of my shirt.

I fell to my knees and immediately discovered that I had both defecated and urinated in my pants. Mother cocked her fist back for another blow and then froze in mid-swing. The streets were silent. An old bible was sitting precariously on the edge of the coffee table, and on the cover was a picture of the boy Jesus. I knelt, waiting for the next blow. The anxiety mounted, and I closed my eyes. Using the defensive skill I had perfected, my mind jumped to a safe place. Nothing happened. Her fist did not connect. It was quiet, except for the sound of Lynn crying – a gut sob that brought up a hitch in her throat every now and then. When I opened my eyes, Mother was standing and staring down at me solemnly. She bent, knees popping and sounding like gunshots when they did. She stroked my face affectionately, and I could not tell if the oily texture of her palm against my cheek was blood or sweat. Then Mother leaned in and gave me a kiss on the forehead, letting me know it was all over.

Mother returned to the couch. She said nothing. Walking in slow shuffling steps, Carter took me to the bathroom and bent me over the sink where he ran cool water and splashed it on my face, flushed and already puffy. The water hurt and felt good at the same time. First pain, then the pleasure of cool relief. He gently patted my face dry with toilet paper. My lip felt heavy and swollen. I went to the bedroom and found Sam – Lynn must have brought him in from outside when she came into the house.

When I picked him up in my arms, his body twitched and he gasped for air. I wasn't sure what had caused it, but I wasn't focusing well at that moment either. It was safe to cry and so I did. The tears stung my eyes.

I slowly turned and sat down on the bed with Sam drawn across my legs, and he stayed that way, his head hung over one of them. The spot where he lay moments before was still warm from his body. I stroked him, feeling the ripple of his ribs. He twitched again and nearly slipped from my lap.

I continued to stare down at Sam, checking for some sign of whatever caused him to shudder. His tiny slit of a mouth opened, and he thankfully offered up a yawn.

The snot, now caked up in my nose from crying, forced me to hold my mouth open in order to breathe. My bottom lip was throbbing. From the living room, I heard Mother speaking to herself and then offering up a guttural chuckle.

Tomorrow, I thought, *I'll steal some milk for Sam from the corner store. He needs to keep his strength up. He's probably just hungry. That's why he shivered. I'll steal him some cheese as well.*

CHAPTER NINE

IT WAS NOT LONG before I realized that Sam was truly sick. Only a few weeks into the new summer, he had lost a significant amount of weight. Soon he began to have convulsions that caused him to shiver uncontrollably and then fall to the floor. There was no money for medicine or veterinary care. There was, however, plenty of money for booze and cigarettes.

Mother was baffled and bemused by how much I cared for Sam. It made her angry. Hanging on to Sam was all I had; it was clean fear that I would lose him. Without Sam, I had only the slow gutting of what was left of me, and the long quiet nights after the molestations, where I sat stinking of her in motionless desolation.

Behind the irony of Sam's illness was the fact that I, too, became ill. I was suffering from something that racked my upper torso with agonizing pain and rendered me paralyzed from the waist down. The affliction came on around the middle of summer.

Wrapped in an old blanket, Sam and I would sit together on the loveseat in the living room for hours. Sam's fur was always soaking wet with the sweat that poured from both our bodies. Once, the neighbor girl who gave me Sam stopped by the house. She was a buxom, jolly-looking girl, and wiped her nose incessantly with the palm of her hand in an upward motion. When she saw Sam and me sitting on the loveseat, filthy and sick, she was horrified and questioned Mother – and got a taste of Mother's nasty mouth. After throwing the neighbor girl out, Mother stood at the doorway, calling her a fat whore. I could hear the girl crying as she ran from the house.

Her name was Saffron, and she was a few years older than me. I once asked her for advice about Sam when he first became ill, but she was not much help. She had given the litter of kittens away, and the mother cat roamed and eventually didn't come back. Saffron knew very little about caring for a sick cat and told me just to try to keep Sam warm. The only other advice Saffron gave me was to get Sam to the vet and to keep him away from Mother.

Lynn had been terribly concerned about both Sam and me. I could not move around much at all, and so Lynn would often help me to the restroom as best she could when the time came. However, because of my excessive sweating, it rarely ever did.

I would have to drag myself along the floor with one arm, while Lynn pulled the other arm forward. Getting up on the toilet itself was difficult, but Lynn and I managed. When Carter was home he would help us too, but he spent more time away when I was sick. Lynn would not leave with him during my illness. It must have been difficult for Carter with a drunken mother and a sick brother in the same house. There would be long, monotonous successions of me just sitting there on the loveseat holding Sam, along with Mother's undeviating assortment of complaints about me being sick. Like me, Carter was limited to the boundaries of being a kid himself, and I couldn't blame him for wanting to leave.

Once when Lynn was helping me down the hall, Mother jumped from her chair and gave my legs a hard kick. I felt nothing, but went rolling briskly to one side of the hallway. She kicked again and again, while Lynn begged her to stop. I noticed Mother's eyes were dreary throughout the entire ordeal. Her face had shown nothing but a lackluster expression – unexcited, dry, and lifeless.

So much of my time was spent on the loveseat when I was sick. While Sam lay with me, wrapped in a blanket in my lap, he would breathe in short shallow rasps. I would occasionally lick my finger and touch his small mouth to be sure the air was moving in and out. The same way I would check Mother when she passed out.

Ironically, I had learned this trick from Mother when she checked on one of her regulars as he slept. His name was Red and he lived on the same block. He was what you would call a 'freebee', if it were not for the cheap wine he exchanged for sex.

Sometimes, he would be passed out in her bed, a hump under the covers, and not even the bedsprings were moving. Therefore, Mother would suck her finger, pulling it from her mouth, making this popping noise, and hold it under his nose. "Son-of-a-bitch is alive," she would say and slap him hard across the face to wake him up.

One morning, while Sam and I sat wrapped in the old blanket, I remember how he stirred, but did not open his eyes – too weak even to preen his fur. Suddenly, he felt like dead weight. His belly no longer moved up and down. "Sam!" I shouted, but he was completely limp.

"Stop fucking with that cat!" Mother screamed.

Without hesitation, I screamed back, "He's dying!"

Nothing reveals courage more than desperation and I was desperate. At the mercy of Mother, I had never even come close to this level of courage until Sam became sick. It was a blind and stupid bravery that was barely within my reach most times, but I grabbed at it frantically.

Lynn jumped up and ran to me. Mother didn't move from where she was sitting. She only watched as this awful scene played out, with the usual stupid look upon her face – dim-witted and faded.

"Sam! Don't die! Don't die, please!" I pleaded.

"Don't talk back to your mother!" she said to no one in particular. It was as if she were responding to a conversation held long before now.

"Same old shit!" Mother went on. "You crying over the fucking cat. Crying and carrying on like a little, queer cocksucker."

Her words went unnoticed as Lynn and I worked on gently moving Sam out from under the blanket, in order to get a better look. I felt distracted because of the panic – sick and hazy.

I looked up at Lynn, kneeling on the floor before me, vigorously moving the soaked covers out of the way. She moved graciously and robustly at the same time. I watched her hands. Unlike mine, they were healthy, calm, capable hands, doing the duties of caring for a cat she loved as well.

"He's breathing! Gregg, he's breathing again!" Lynn shouted, which came out *"bweathing."*

Mother lunged toward me, shoving Lynn aside. Now, standing directly in front of me and glaring downward, she rocked back and forth with a drunken sway, but said nothing.

I did not look up. I continued to check and re-check what Lynn had shouted. That was all that mattered.

When Mother finally spoke, her voice had a menacing smoothness to it. "I'm going to strangle Sam when you're asleep. When you wake up tomorrow, he'll be dead." I saw she was smiling, satisfied with herself.

"Please don't, Mommy. I'm sorry." I said, but that only seemed to make her angrier.

In an instant, Mother sprang for me. I had just enough time to move Sam to one side. Even then, I marveled at her physical strength, while she pulled me upward by the hair and then let go. Without any muscle control in my legs, I came crashing down atop the coffee table, bounced upward again, and then fell to the floor. My eyes never left Sam, who was now looked lifeless on the loveseat only a few inches from me.

"Here's your fucking sorry!" Mother bellowed directly into my ear. "Here's your fucking sorry!" she screamed again, and the smell of alcohol-saturated breath filled my face.

I continued to lay still, keeping a close watch on Sam. Done in, my head felt like it weighed a thousand pounds; I simply gave in and let it fall to the floor, waiting for Mother to stop screaming into my face. When she did, Lynn helped me to my knees and eventually back on to the loveseat. After making sure I was settled, she placed Sam on my lap. Like me, he was wet and shivering.

My head hurt something awful, and I could see Lynn's eyes were raw from crying.

"Sam's okay," I said and pulled his body closer to my stomach.

Looking at him now, I couldn't believe he was the same kitten. His face looked desolate, almost blank. I couldn't bear the thought of being without him and tried to cry as quietly as possible. Mother was only a few feet away, and although she seemed to be drifting off from drinking, she was capable of coming out of a stupor in a matter of seconds. Sometimes, as she sat there staring at us, her face would seem to change shape, and would go from lifeless to alert. From tranquil to dangerous, and we knew she was about to go into a rage. I couldn't let that happen again. Not now – not with Sam so sick. He'd die for sure without me.

As I laid my hand under his paw, letting it rest on top of a couple of my fingers, just for a moment I felt something strange go through me. The feeling had something to do with why I was fighting so hard for Sam.

I ran my fingers up his back and stopped where there was a collar around his neck. It was something I had made, a green ribbon laced through a St. Christopher medal I had stolen from Kyle. Months ago, I had slipped the decoration over his lovely face onto his neck. It was a perfect fit. However now, it was far too big, and if Sam could have stood on his own, it would have hung all the way to the floor.

I faintly stroked the downy soft hair under Sam's chin. Mother had gone into one of the bedrooms and passed out. Lynn had fallen asleep in one of the chairs, and the house was uncommonly quiet. From outside, through a crack in one of the windows, I heard the wind. It sounded like a high-pitched, haunting laugh.

CHAPTER TEN

FALL WAS APPROACHING and with it school would follow, and with school, more shame. As I looked out of the window, there was an ache in the small of my back – a place that, up until this moment, had been nerveless. It passed, and my attention was drawn to Sam again where he was cradled like a baby in the crook of my folded arms.

Revolting thoughts began racing through my mind in increasing numbers, and Sam was among them. I tried not to look too closely, but they were drawing nearer in clarity. Hope was growing faint.

Suddenly, I became aware that Mother was standing at the end of the dark hallway.

"I knew you were faking it, you little cocksucker," Mother said furiously.

I realized immediately what she meant. I was standing. The ability to do so had come back so suddenly and unexpectedly that I did not realize I had stood up with Sam in my arms.

Mother quickly moved the down the short hallway and pounced. I half-threw, half-dropped Sam onto the loveseat. The blanket he was wrapped in broke his fall. My arms were flailing in order keep balanced, but it was no use. I had not walked in several weeks, and my legs were weak. I spun around and was yanked backward, forcing me into a kneeling position, facing the same window I was staring out only minutes ago.

From behind me and snatching a lock of my hair, Mother snapped my head backward. I saw Sam from my peripheral vision, and he seemed to be convulsing under the blanket, his movements jerky.

Mother shouted, "Faker!" – and walked back into the bedroom where she had probably left her drink. Forcing myself to kneel upright again, I felt sharp pains in my legs and back. Sam was no longer convulsing. His eyes were only slits. His mouth closed. His head lay over one paw and dipped slightly. I could see his belly moving rapidly up, in, and out. I gathered him up in my arms, blanket and all, and sat back down on the loveseat. I put my finger to his small chest and felt his heart was pounding as fast as mine.

The paralysis was gone. The pain in my legs told me that. I looked at my hand, and it was bleeding. It must have hit the sharp corner of the coffee table.

My eyes grew heavy. Mother would be back soon, Sam was getting worse, but I was so tired. I looked again at my hand and fell off to sleep.

Just before school started, the paralysis had ended. Sam was getting worse. I would rush home from school to take care of him and would spend much time sitting with him asleep on my lap. Fall turned into winter, and there was a chill in the house. The utility company had shut off our heat, claiming they had not received payment from the State.

Near fall, the house was always cold and in the winter, it was freezing. The kind of cold that hurts all the way down to the bone. The wind blew in from outside and all over the house. You could hear it whistle and moan. We would stuff shirts and towels around the windows to keep out the cold as best we could. Sometimes, Mother would turn on the gas oven and open its door. My siblings and I would huddle together on the kitchen linoleum floor, before its black mouth agape and hissing, and relish in its warm breath.

Sitting Indian-style on the loveseat with Sam on my lap, I pulled the blanket up around my shoulders. Sam stirred and made a wheezing noise. While holding him, I looked out the small living room window and noticed there was a fresh dusting of frost that covered the ground like a white apron. There was also frost on the window. Evening had set in, and I remember the warmth between me and my kitty compared to how cold it looked outside.

An icy Midwestern wind was blowing, and I began quietly singing. "Mary had a little lamb, little lamb, little lamb – Mary had a little lamb. Its fleece was white as snow." It was a tune I learned on an old player piano we had in the basement. While singing, I continued looking out the window, watching moonlit snowflakes beginning to fall. "Everywhere that Mary went – the lamb was sure to go."

It was really snowing now, and there was already a small curve of powder built up at the base of one of the bottom exterior panes. The window appeared to be smiling at me. Afraid Sam would get too warm, I moved the blanket off of him. My eyes would go from the window to Sam, and back again – watching for some sort of movement. Some sign of the life he used to have. I suppose it was hope I was looking for.

I knew he was dying. At the very least, I wanted to be there when he did. I began to feel lately that even this would not be possible. It was a fear that came from a bottomless place, deep within my heart.

Winter passed. Spring was here, and it would be summer soon. This meant I would be able to spend all day with Sam, nursing him back to health. He had survived the winter, which meant there was a chance he was going to make it and I had survived another difficult school year. Once school was out, he would no longer be left all alone with Mother. Every day I would rush home from school and find Sam exactly where I had left him on the loveseat. I had returned to feeding Sam with the eyedropper, as I did when he was just born. Eventually he stopped eating altogether, and the convulsions became more prominent and longer lasting.

On the last day of school, I ran all the way home without stopping to catch my breath, even though my lungs burned. Although Lynn shouted for me to wait up, I did not listen. I cleared the two porch steps and ran through the front door relieved to know with school out of the way, I could spend every day caring for Sam.

The blanket he normally was wrapped in was there on the loveseat, but Sam was not. Mother sat on the couch drunk, and it was how she looked at me that I knew something was wrong. Mother's singular practice of lifting the booze cup to her mouth seemed difficult. She was extremely uncomfortable from the outset, and her voice shook as much as her hand holding the cup. I thought for a moment it was the sickness coming on, but then I again looked at the empty blanket, and before she mouthed the words, I said them aloud. "Sam's dead" – and forgetting her rule about showing emotion, I wept in front of her and would go on weeping until my chest ached.

I remember the dull ignorance on her face, and how Mother's eyes looked more guilty than ashamed or sorry. There were long pauses in between each question I asked and each was the same. "What happened to Sam?"

She seemed to ponder the question seriously as if it were not the same question I had just asked, but she did not answer me. Mother just went on staring at the floor and sipping her wine. Then she regained the balance of power that always served to place her world back on an even plane. Mother took back control and quickly dismissed me from the room with one angry threat. There could be little doubt something terrible lied beneath the surface of what happened to Sam. I would never know, and the only creature that made me feel just a little safe was now gone.

I lay on my bed and cried, desperately wishing Mother was just playing a cruel joke and Sam was hidden somewhere in the house. He was not. Not knowing how he died made it worse. It was important to me that he did not suffer in the end. It became difficult to keep Sam within my thoughts without the anger interfering and pushing away the images of his playful character. Several nights were spent lying awake and trying to remember him. Daydreaming about what he once was by closing my eyes and concentrating. I would hold the image of him for a few seconds, and then it would disappear, but not before I glimpsed his small face slipping slowly away in front of mine.

PART THREE
When I Was a Child

"Where does one go from a world of insanity?
Somewhere on the other side of despair."

T.S. Eliot

CHAPTER ELEVEN

I LEFT THE CORNER STORE, walking past the first house and toward home. The flesh on my arms still burned from the lit matches tossed at me by the storekeeper. He was a stout old cuss. Most of the time he was businesslike, but he had caught me stealing again. I tried to drop the booty in my pants pocket when I thought he wasn't looking, then I casually walked up to the counter and asked for a piece of penny candy as a decoy. But he figured the bulge in my pocket had not been there when I walked into the store. As I stood there waiting for the penny candy, he grabbed a box of wooden matches, and with hands like a skilled surgeon, he dragged one match after another across the striker, lighting and throwing them in one smooth motion.

The matches cleared the rubber change mat lying on the counter, doing tiny flips in the air, igniting and then landing painfully on the exposed flesh of my arm. Most of them just stung a little, then bounced off. However a few stuck to the skin and burned.

By the time he waddled around the counter to give chase, I was already out the exit. He always stopped short at the end of the parking lot, so once I crossed the street connecting to our block, I was home free.

When I got closer to the house, my stomach was grumbling in anticipation of the hard-earned fruit pie in my pocket. I noticed as I got closer to home that there was an unfamiliar car in the driveway. *Mother must be entertaining*, I thought, and continued past our house and down the street. It had been a year since Mother had been in the hospital, and she now operated back at her normal speed, bringing the men in and out regularly.

I walked with my head down, keeping to the middle of the sidewalk, pretending either side was a steep drop into a fathomless chasm. When I reached the end of the block, I looked up momentarily to cross the street and headed for the grouping of trees and undergrowth we referred to as "the field." Turning slightly to the left, the ground beneath my feet went from asphalt to willow brush and eventually, green grass. Leading to a storm drain was a narrow river. I watched the swirling brown water carry away a smattering of small twigs and buds where they would disappear into an iron mouth, making me think of the fruit pie in my pocket. Apple, my favorite.

I stood on the metal plate and listened to the water dump into the drain. Stamped beneath my worn sneakers were the words *Water and Sewer*. I stepped off the drain and walked further into the field. As I walked, the grass became thicker and taller. The trees grew larger and closer together. The air was cool, almost chilly, and I felt more at peace.

Only a few minutes before, I had narrowly escaped with the fruit pie. The son-of-a-bitch storeowner was a mean bastard, and I knew he would have hurt me worse had he been able to catch me. The old man was slow, but he had a double-barrel shotgun hidden behind the counter. I knew this for a fact because it'd been pointed at my mother a few times when she got to cussing him out if she thought he cheated her out of a couple bucks. She'd just go on cussing at him, waving her arms all over the place as if he wasn't standing there with a loaded gun in her face. I'd beg her to leave, tugging on her arm. The old man had this thick Hungarian accent and would bark, "Listen to ya boy, friggen whore, and move on." This went on about every couple weeks, but he kept selling his booze to her and Mother kept buying it.

The wind started to pick up, and the sky turned a little darker. I kept walking on through the field. I thought of turning back, but I knew it wouldn't be safe. Not that it ever was, but if Mother had a man in her bed, I didn't want to be around. The shame was unbearable. I had learned that, when the men came over, things got worse than usual. The thing to do was to get the hell out of the house. Then, if I took a beating for not being around to skim their wallets, it was better than watching them lay on her and make those awful grunting sounds. I still couldn't tell time or tie my own shoes, but I was smart enough to know trouble when I saw it.

The sky was now completely black, and by the time I reached the trees, it was as if it went from day to night in only a few seconds. It was going to storm, there was no doubt of that now, and I had no place to go. I settled next to a thick oak and waited for the rain.

In the distance, lightning lit up the clouds, then thunder rolled. I was told that you wanted to steer clear of a tree during a lightning storm. I jerked and curled into a ball. I could smell electricity in the air. Another snap of light shot across the sky followed by a crash of thunder so loud it made me scream. Suddenly, the rain came, and it felt like needles against my skin. Thunder cracked again overhead and the wind blew harder. More rain needled and stung my face. It came down so hard I could not see anything in front of me. Nothing but wet blindness and hard cold rain.

I was now completely drenched and freezing. The lightning strikes grew farther apart, but the rain was coming down harder than ever. Several small puddles formed all around me. *I'll wait out the storm*, I thought. *Just like with Mother*. It was both relieving and heart-breaking at the same time.

I didn't want to get hurt anymore. But I didn't want to leave Mother. Yet she tortured me. She let Sam die, and the rage against her for this boiled inside me, mixed with bitter confusion. The rain continued to fall, and I wondered if I was going crazy. I closed my eyes and wondered if this was finally the end.

It was a fear of mine to go completely insane. A fear Mother would perpetuate by telling me that I was already very close to total lunacy. "Your grandfather went crazy, you know?" she would say with a glint in her eye. "He lost his fucking mind and died in a mental institution. You know your grandfather had to wear one of those straitjackets because he would try to dig his eyes out and punch himself in the balls."

At this, she would swing at my genitals and sometimes make contact, causing me to fall to the floor gasping for air. She would then lean over me and whisper, "Gregg, you look just like your grandfather."

I once saw a picture of my grandfather when he was only a boy. It scared me something awful, because she was right. I looked just like him.

When the rain slowed to a drizzle, I got up and began walking back home, forgetting about the fruit pie in my pocket. Escaping to Lauren's didn't seem real anymore. It had been over a year since the option first came up, but nothing had progressed. Yet I never lost the will to survive. Not because I was courageous or brave. It was simply because I knew nothing else.

As I passed the houses, I could hear the pinging and rattling of the rain against the gutters. About halfway home, I noticed the unfamiliar car was gone and hoped that Mother was content with what the man had paid her. It would be even better if she were passed out, and I could sneak inside and quietly change into dry clothes. My hopes were soon replaced with agony when I saw the screen door burst open and Mother step out onto the porch. She eyed me immediately and stared without saying a word. Her mouth was a thin line. Her arms crossed. My only hope now was that both Carter and Lynn were home. However, it would not have mattered if they were.

I continued walking along the sidewalk toward the house. The sidewalk was not steep, but it felt steep to me. My legs became heavy with dread. In front of me was a puddle, and I sloshed through it without care not to get my shoes wet. I was already sopping wet, anyway.

I passed the house next to ours. There was a dog, as wet as I was, hitched to a stake in the yard. It looked at me distrustingly when I passed by, and I instinctively put my hands in my pockets in case he jumped forward and nipped at my fingers. My impulse proved correct. The dog put its ears back and showed its teeth, then barked, and jerked its head. The distance closed between me and Mother and my fear increased.

I walked further along the sidewalk, slowing my pace. My head down, I then turned right and into our front yard. In my mind, I tried to think of the field and how it stretched outward, away from the houses, becoming open country. How the blue of the sky was more prominent over the vastness of the field. It helped a little, but not much. I could feel Mother's eyes glaring down from the porch on me, and something caught in my throat.

The protection of the field was behind me. *I could turn back and run*, I thought. I could run until I reached the trees of the field and keep on running. On the other side of the field, I thought there must be a better place. Where I could start again. Like when we fouled up our turn during a game of tag and asked for a "do-over." Yes. That's what I needed most. A "do-over."

Before nearly reaching the porch, Mother started for me. I realized that I should have stayed in the field, despite the storm. I had been safe there. I was no longer moving, frozen in place, expecting the worst. There was a loud bang, which I thought was more thunder, but then the left side of my face exploded. What followed was a grand sweeping of landscape before I came crashing to the ground.

She pulled me up by the hair and dragged me a few feet over to the porch. I was forced down hard, and upon smacking my tailbone, a series of electric jabs went shooting up my spine. Mother remained absolutely silent. No yelling. No cursing. She sat down next to me and looked out over the yard. When she finally spoke, her tone was calm. "You're lucky to be alive. The lightning could have killed you." She then turned her face toward me and whispered in my ear. "This isn't over, goddamnit." Mother got up and walked inside, her voice moving away as she did.

Mother was the crazy kind that you saw coming at you staggering, shouting obscenities, and flailing her arms, but she was also the crazy kind that was calculating and manipulative. This made her the most dangerous kind of crazy there was.

Worse than when you saw it coming was when you did not. That was when Mother was planning the beating in her head. She would sit on the couch, always with a cigarette smoldering next to her. Always with a drink in her hand or within reach, staring at nothing, and then she would fix on me.

Sometimes, she would start off in a conversational tone with a question that didn't make much sense: "Gregg, whose side are you on?" Her voice would be dry and clear without a trace of awareness.

"I'm on your side, Mamma," I would reply, and then she would just go on looking at me. She would then tell me that she loved me, and I believed it, because I was afraid. I was willing to believe a lot of things, especially when I desperately wanted them to be true.

Then she would tell me to come and sit next to her, and I would. Our arms and legs would be right up against one another, and sometimes we would both be wearing shorts and no sleeves. Skin against skin, which made me ashamed and sick in my stomach.

Mother would then turn and look at my face, and sometimes she would kiss me on the mouth. I would get a sick feeling. Then her hot and dry hand would come crashing against my cheek, and I'd be drowned in brilliant purple light, hidden behind a curtain of both surprise and heart-wrenching fear.

Afterwards, she would tell me to go away from her and sit down on the floor. Looking at her, you would never know she just slapped me if it were not for the cords standing out in her neck. Mother would go back to looking at nothing, sometimes with this peaceful smile, and I would try really hard not to cry and make her mad.

I had honestly begun to wonder if the alcohol destroyed Mother's brain and made her crazy, or if she had been that way before she started drinking. If she had been crazy all along, maybe she had gotten it from her father. Then that meant it could happen to me. It terrified me more than the abuse did. Mother could pass on her insanity to me. I wondered with genuine fear if crazy was catching.

There was a brief moment while sitting on the porch when I allowed myself a fantasy about heading back toward the field along with its defending grove of trees. The moment passed. I got up to go inside. The fear and hatred for her grew stronger. Rage burned inside of me, but yet again, I would obey Mother. I was caught somewhere between two worlds: hatred and helpless devotion.

By the time the screen door banged shut, I was yanked to the carpet. Mother shouted, "What is your name?" It was just another trick question. One that I would never get right and would provide her with the minimum justification necessary to carry out what she was about to do. "Your name, goddamnit! What is your name!"

I said nothing, knowing that any answer would prove useless. A hard slap and then another – both landing to the side of my face Mother had struck only minutes before when I first stepped into the yard. She was directly behind me, holding my head upright by a clump of my hair. Another slap and another, and the last caused me to twist and pull something in my back. She landed another blow to the same side of my face. Cupping her hand slightly, Mother hit me again, forcing a suction around my ear – driving the air inward.

The pain was excruciating. Something popped inside my head, and the sound of her voice suddenly changed, becoming muffled.

Multicolored lights and starbursts danced inside my head. My ear rang, drowning out her shouts. I just closed my eyes and concentrated on the field. I concentrated and waited for her to stop. The thought of losing my mind came rushing back. *What if she gives me brain damage?* I wondered.

Mother had been holding her cigarette pinched between her middle and forefinger in the hand pulling my hair. As she rolled her knuckles forward to get a better grip, the cigarette rolled forward as well. The lit ash, now tangled within my hair, burned at my scalp, and I frantically slapped at my own skull. Mother stopped. Perhaps, my display of self-abuse had caused her to do so. She did not sit down on the couch. Instead, she left the room and headed for the bedroom where she had recently been with the stranger. Mother was probably making sure the money she collected was still there after the bitter exchange of drunken sex.

My body ached all over. Using the coffee table as leverage, I pulled myself up and went over to a chair to sit down. Once sitting, I laid the right side of my head down on the armrest. The left side felt twice its normal size and hurt. My mind drifted off, looking for some sort of foothold on reality. I thought about Lauren again. It gave me some comfort and got my mind off the pain. I began thinking that it wouldn't be a silly plan of escape or fantasy any longer – I'd make sure of that.

I forced myself to get up from the chair and go to the kitchen to find some ice in the freezer. I shoved a few cubes in one of my socks and made an icepack for my face. I snuck out the back door and went over to the apple tree. I had to fight the dreadful feelings of remorse when they crept up inside my head. Settling down on the old crate with the sock filled with ice against my cheek, I let myself fall into one of my favorite make-believe games of being a soldier. Sometimes I'd act it out with a fake rifle, scurrying around the field or construction site behind the corner store. Other times, I would sit alone and just imagine. Especially under the protective cover of the apple tree.

But I knew deep down that I was not a soldier. I followed Mother's orders blindly, and I was a soldier in that regard. I also bled and therefore I was like a soldier. I was not brave, but I did not believe all soldiers were. I believed, like me, a lot of them just followed orders and hoped they were not hurt or killed. Yet hard-boiled into them was all that training, and I had none of that. It was just make-believe for me, and not real like the pain in my cheek. I was not a solider at all. I was only a kid, and the fantasy of being a soldier was fading and funneling away.

I raised my head in order to look out through the thick growth of leaves. There was a single line of apples hanging neatly across one of the branches. Looking down again near my feet, I noticed an arc of sunlight. I thought, *If Sam were here, he'd be staring at it and every now and then swat at it with his paw.* This made me smile, sending a jolt of pain across my entire face. I watched the arc of sunlight grow narrow, thin to a mere slit, and then fade away entirely as a cloud drifted by briefly. Rising slowly, I walked through the natural opening, stooping as I went, and stood up when I reached the outer skirt of the apple tree. My back protested and made random popping sounds – already beginning to stiffen.

It was cool, and for a moment, it felt as if fall was coming. Summer would be over soon, and I would be starting school. It would be my last year attending elementary and then on to junior high. I was not ready for the higher academics and suddenly felt embarrassed. But this meant nothing to me now compared to what my life was at home.

I would walk back to the field tomorrow and find a quiet place deep within the trees. Far away from where the older kids hung out and smoked their joints.

I knew Mother would be angry when I returned home. She would give me that craning look when I walked into the house, and her jawbone would be slowly working over the butt of her non-filtered *Kools Menthol* cigarette. Her eyelids would be half-lowered and working me over slowly too, like her cigarette. Still, I hoped maybe she'd be passed out and wouldn't notice when I came home.

I headed toward the back door. She still needed me, I knew that, but not the way a good mother needs a son. As I reached for the screen door, this fresh and liberating feeling came back to me, stronger than ever. It did not matter if Mother needed me. I began to realize I did not need her.

CHAPTER TWELVE

Throughout that night, it felt as though my heart was frozen. There was no love and no hate. My mind walked into and out of all those things that once kept me resolute in my decision never to leave her. I was close to breaking free. Closer than I had ever been before. Freedom was within reach for the first time in my life. I could feel it. It was as if I was breaking through a new-formed crust of ice into a pool of cool, fresh water. I lay down and fell fast asleep thinking of leaving Mother for good.

Morning came, and with it, her rage. Mother had found the scratch paper that I had written my master plan upon: "Call Jessica frum corner store. Tell her com git us. Go live with Lauren." I had put the words down over a year ago and read them over and over. They gave me a goal, something to live for without Sam.

My head was still on the pillow when her hand came down and busted me in the nose. I tasted blood running down the back of my throat, making me gag and swallow rapidly. I could see she was holding my plan in the same hand that crashed into my nose. She was past comprehension and far from restraint. She was screaming something, but it rang hollow against my ears.

Mother climbed on top of me, pinning me down. This always struck me as peculiar because I never fought back. She grabbed my lower lip and pulled hard. The pain pushed me into a dark tunnel. All of a sudden, my testicles felt as though they were on fire. Mother had reached back, taken hold of them, and squeezed. In an instant, day turned into night and everything stopped momentarily. Mother climbed off me and left the room.

Carter suddenly ran into the bedroom and to my side of the bed. His voice came from very far away and sounded crippled and broken. I was curled into a fetal position, holding my testicles and struggling to breathe. Carter's voice was raspy and echoes of his voice were ringing in my ears, but I could not move. I could not see. For several agonizing moments, I found myself trapped between sleep and wakefulness.

Carter sat down on the bed next to me while I gasped for air. Gradually, the ache in my groin subsided, and the air again moved easily in and out of my lungs.

"I'm all right," I told Carter; however, when I swung my legs out onto the floor, the room swam temporarily. "I'm going for a walk," I said and thankfully was able to sneak out the front door while Mother was in the kitchen, pouring herself another glass of wine or whatever rotgut she was drinking. My testicles ached as I walked down the street and toward the field.

The warmth of the sun felt good. My plan was to first rest a bit in the field, and then later I'd cut through the old apartments on the other side of the block in order to avoid my house on my way to the corner store. In my pocket was thirty cents, enough to purchase a soda and fruit pie, and I was relieved to know I wouldn't have to steal this time. Back in the trees, I would eat and sleep.

Upon the reaching the field, I hummed "Mary had a little lamb," as I walked, allowing my hand, palm down, to brush the tops of the Indian Grass. Once on the smooth green blades that led up to the taller weeds, under the bright sunshine, I stopped and closed my eyes, enjoying the warmth on my tender nose. I left the soft weeds, and they whispered against my shoes as I headed for the trees. For now, I would sit against one of the tall oaks and rest. The sky was a beautiful bloom of bluish white.

I had spent the whole day in the field, leaving only once to get the fruit pie and soda. It was growing darker now, and realizing I had spent a considerable amount of time away from Mother without panicking or fretting to the point where I would go running back to her, filled me with surprised joy. Along the darkening street, I made my way home. My heart became stiff and cold the closer I came to the house.

There was a chill in the air that told me I would catch hell, and remembering Mother had found the note with the plan written on it enforced this belief. I'd still have to pay for my disloyal behavior with more beatings. Apprehensive about going home, I walked on the opposite side of the street. Closer to the house, a phantom pain shot through my groin, and I suddenly halted when I saw Mother sitting on the porch, smoking a cigarette. I could tell when she took a drag because the tip would glow very bright and then subside. *She is waiting for me*, I thought.

A car turned the corner, and I ducked behind Kyle's house and hid away for a second. With all the strength I had, I walked across the street and out of the shielding darkness. My tongue probed the raw split in my lip nervously. When I reached the steps of the porch, Mother flicked her cigarette into the yard and got up to go inside. I knew that was the signal for me to follow her in.

I waited until she shut the screen door before I opened it. I then went into the house. It was dark, but Mother lit a match to ignite another cigarette. When she did, the glow cast a shadow of her head against the wall, and I thought of the paper cutout of an old style portrait we had once made of ourselves in school. There were two profiles depicting the left and right sides of my head. They were facing one another within a folded piece of paper. Mother tore it up in front of me saying it was a queer thing to do. It had been a gift to her on Mother's Day.

"Come here," Mother said and stood up. She reached out her hand and told me to take it. I was led down the hallway and into her bedroom. She told me to strip down, climb onto the bed, and get under the covers. They stank of sex. Mother followed after me. The metal springs under the mattress squeaked as she climbed in the bed. When she slid next to my body, I could feel she was naked, and her skin felt cold. "Take off those goddamn underwear," she whispered.

She leaned to one side and hoisted herself up, resting on her elbow facing me. I pushed my underwear down to my ankles and used my feet to kick them off the rest of the way. Mother was still smoking her cigarette. Taking one last puff, she crushed it against the headboard. It was pitch-black, and I could hear her exhale the last of the smoke that filled her lungs.

Her hand moved to my genitals, and cupping them whole, she squeezed. Although she did so much more gently than before, they still ached, and I felt the sickness rise up in my throat, choking me. "You're not going to leave Mommy, are you?" she said.

I could hear her breathing quicken. Without a single utterance and while she forced me to please her sexually for what seemed an eternity, in my heart I answered her.

The molestations had been going on for years, but they seemed worse for me as I got older. My mind was not able to justify, nor comprehend, what took place in Mother's bed. Reason stopped dead against a wall of shame and confusion, and there was no punching through it. No answers to any of the abuse as to why. Only a sharp reminder, every time she raped me, that I was one more step closer to complete and total insanity. Soon, I thought, a trap-door deep within my mind would be raised, and the horror I'd kept locked up all these years would climb through.

In the corner of my mind, there was a mirror, and the reflection was not my face, but something distorted and angry. It took great effort to push the sight away; however, the rage building inside of me was becoming even more powerful. What was once love became hate.

I was running out of strength. It was nearly used up. Leaving me too was the desire to help my siblings. I knew one day it would be gone. I knew I had to act soon. I would figure out a way to escape this place. All I had to do was convince Lauren.

The sex acts became more frequent and brutal. Mother then got it in her head that she could up the ante on prostituting herself if she got the teenage boys in the neighborhood involved. She did and they came and went.

The teen boys were more particular when it came to a mate. More so than the old comely drunks Mother usually attracted. Therefore, doomed by her usual appearance of being grotesquely skinny and generally unwashed, Mother resorted to an inventive array of other sexual practices. Those that did not involve penetration.

The boys that took part in this disgusting ritual would tease me when we passed on the sidewalk, "blow jobs and hand jobs…the only job your mother has." During their taunts, I also learned that apparently it was the same price for both.

There was no cause for the increase in the molestations, except maybe the fact I was getting older. However, they did increase and it was not just with Mother.

He was a short and fat man. One of Mother's regulars. I had been sitting under the apple tree, blissfully alone. The ground, kept cool from the shade of the branches, was soft under my bare feet. I took in deep breaths and let them out slowly in order to calm me down; something I did often. I leaned against the trunk of the apple tree and closed my eyes. Before long, I was asleep.

The sound of the back door slamming shut woke me. Peering through the branches, I saw the fat man with beady little eyes, balding and always wet with perspiration. He was walking toward me. How could he have known about my hiding place? And as if to answer, from the open kitchen window, floating through the air, came the haunting sound of Mother's laughter.

"You must be Gregg," the man said on his hands and knees, pushing through the foliage. I immediately scooted away from him, putting the trunk between the two of us. He had on a red-and-white striped shirt that was too tight, and bent over with his gut hanging down he looked like a fat candy cane. "Your momma and me want you back in the house," he said, suddenly lunging for me. I squirmed out the other side of the tree, scraping up my arms on the rough bark of the branches and ran. By the time I reached the sidewalk, I was crying, but didn't stop running.

When I thought it was safe to return home, I did. The man was gone, and Mother sat drinking. She didn't say a word, but I knew she sent the man out to see me. And I knew why. What I didn't know was how much he had paid her.

That night, Mother went to bed and told me to stay up. Confused at first, I simply obeyed, taking it as a good sign she wasn't making me go to bed with her. About an hour later, there was a soft knock on the door. I went to the window and looked out. It was the candy cane man, and he was wearing the same striped shirt. I stood frozen, and he knocked again. It was no use. Sooner or later, I would be forced to give him what he had already paid for. I unlocked the door, opened it slowly, and he limped inside. I realized I had not noticed the limp earlier that day.

"Please, mister…" I begged, crying.

He leaned down and whispered to keep quiet. Before the man shut the door, I stole a look outside as if to run, and he gripped my shirt with his free hand. It was cold outside. The night was clear. The stars were out.

With his arm around my shoulders, the man led me over to the couch. He sat down and pulled down my underwear, which was all I had on. Grasping my buttocks with his hand, he then knelt in front of me and began sucking at my limp penis. I prayed it would not get erect, and my prayers were answered. This didn't stop the man. It didn't seem to faze him at all. He pulled out his own penis from his pants, which was big and stiff. With his mouth on me, he began rubbing it up and down with his other hand. By now, I was sobbing, my sight blurry with tears, but I tried to keep quiet. Both fear and shame overwhelmed me. Moments later, the man shot a stream of goop. He hurriedly wiped it up with his shirt. "Don't cry," was all he said and quickly and quietly left the house.

The house was dark. A thin slit of light came from the place where the curtains came together, where Carter and I often stood staring out the window and waiting for our father. I could still feel the man's saliva wet and cold on my penis and testicles. The embarrassment was too much to handle, and I wept for several minutes. With what little strength I had left, I got up from the couch, pulled on my underwear, and walked down the hallway toward the room I shared with my brother.

Upon passing Mother's bedroom, came the haunting sound of her laughter.

PART FOUR
The Passing

"Although the world is full of suffering, it is full also of the overcoming of it."

Helen Keller

CHAPTER THIRTEEN

A FEW WEEKS LATER, I walked down the street with my arm slung around Lynn's tiny shoulders. Carter was walking along beside us. The small display of affection made Lynn uncomfortable. We weren't allowed to touch one another – Mother's rule.

The hot sun. The tacky houses of the neighborhood. The three of us walking and not saying a word. Our heads down. Not knowing where we were going. Believing there was no place to go. And coming to understand fully that there was nothing left except to escape.

I shared with my siblings what I'd recently overheard when Jessica had been over – something that had filled me with new hope – or more accurately, what seemed to be our last hope. "Jessica said she got a hold of Lauren," I said. "All we have to do is call Jessica if Mom beats us one more time."

"Fuck man, that won't take long," Carter said and added, "For fuck's sake, Jake . . . that's a fact, Jack."

Lynn giggled and pushed my arm off. I could see a flash of hope in her eyes when she turned to do so. "So what do we do?" Lynn asked while we kept walking. Walking further away from the house and toward the field. I knew I'd miss the field, but that was all.

"All we have to do is wait for next time," I said.

I didn't have the nerve to share my plan with them. I'd draw Mother into a beating frenzy. I'd then run to the store and call Jessica. It didn't matter Mother found my note because she'd play right into it. She'd have no choice. There was no way Mother could stop herself from two things: drinking and hitting me. This time, I was going to use them to get us out of here.

Suddenly, at the end of the block, before it began the gradual curve to the left, Lynn stopped. "I don't want to live with Mom anymore," she said and started to cry.

The strain was too much, and I yelled, "Shut the fuck up!"

Carter was quick to defend her: "You shut the fuck up, Gregg! I'll kick your ass!"

Normally, I would have let it go, however, things were different now. "Fuck you, fatso!" I said and stood my ground.

Carter landed the first punch squarely at the tip of my shoulder. My arm went numb, but I found the strength to swing back. By the time we dropped to the ground, punching, kicking, and biting one another, Lynn was halfway home. Carter pushed himself off me and ran after her, more afraid she'd inadvertently tell Mother what just happened, as opposed to making sure she was all right.

I pulled myself up and headed for the field. When I swung around again to see if Carter and Lynn might have come back, I saw they were gone. Maybe they went inside the house or ducked in the backyard. I didn't care. My arm hurt like hell, and I kept swinging it back and forth to work out the charley horse.

The pavement ended, dropping off slightly, and turned into dirt. The sensation always made me feel better. It told me I was close. Casting a golden light across the field was a late afternoon sun. I grunted and pressed forward. My arm hurt. But I had something to preoccupy my mind. I had a plan to carry out.

Just before the lip of the tree line, before the first thicket of oak and maple, I saw something that turned my beautiful haven into something degenerate. Something so awful that I would never again be able to enjoy the peace this coppice of trees once gave me. Aside from the molestations I had been forced to endure from Mother and strangers, it was the most horrible sight I have ever seen.

Her name was Marla. Prepubescent beauty enveloped her. Long brown hair and eyes to match. She was a classmate of mine, and I had a crush on her from the day I saw her beautiful smile on the playground at school.

She was not smiling now. The neighborhood twin boys, both older than Marla by five or six years, were hurting her. Although she seemed to partake in this revolting ordeal, I could see the anguish in her face. I knew it well. It stared back at me in the mirror.

The twins wore shirts and no pants. Marla was completely naked. They took turns. One boy held her upright while the other would thrust his hips between her legs, spread apart by his brother. She made small groaning sounds and looked up at the sky. There was nothing but a blank expression on her face. I didn't run for help. Who would I tell? Who would care? Instead, I sat low to the ground and watched the rape unfold before me. I did nothing. I said nothing. I was not a hero. Only a stupid boy.

The first twin uttered what sounded very much like a growl, and on his face, he bore an expression of what appeared to be pain. He switched places, and the second twin mimicked the first – in much less time. The twins hurriedly got dressed and ran away laughing.

Still frozen in place, I watched Marla use a pair of crumpled panties to wipe around her crotch. Upon seeing this, I fought the urge to puke by repeatedly swallowing the acid that raced up the back of my throat. She then got dressed, but much more slowly than the twins. Her movements were mechanical. She wasn't crying. Afterwards, she walked directly toward the spot where I was crouched down in the thick tall grass, and turning slightly toward the neighborhood, she missed me by only a few feet.

I breathed a sigh of relief when she passed by. She didn't seem to notice me, and I thought she probably would not have seen me if I was standing directly in front of her. I waited until she left the field and rounded the corner of the block. I had no idea we lived so close to one another. When Marla disappeared out of sight completely, I stood and walked toward home. The trees no longer symbolized the magic they once held. My haven ruined. What good was it to me now?

The apple tree had been spoiled by the stranger who liked little boys. The grove of trees tainted by the rape of a girl I knew. Sam was dead. Leaving this living nightmare was the only solution.

On the way home, a horde of birds flew overhead, seeking the protection and tranquility of the field and its trees. I felt a pang of regret stab me in the gut and thought of Marla.

My thoughts went to the reminders of sex I tried to bury, but they always surfaced. I pushed hard to keep them away, but the thoughts would push back and come in a rush.

Mother, the sex, and then the floodgates would open. The stranger's mouth on me. The babysitter with her underwear around her ankles, kneeling and sucking so hard it hurt.

We were often left alone while Mother was out drinking with one of the many people in the neighborhood that drank as well. Although it never seemed to me that they drank as much as her. Sometimes, when Mother was at Mrs. Dowling's, her youngest daughter, Sachi would come over to the house. She would say that Mother had sent her to check on us, but I knew better. Mother would have never cared enough to have anyone come and check on us. She never would have even thought of it.

Sachi was probably sixteen or seventeen. A plump girl who liked to wear shirts cut off just under her breasts with no bra and her belly hung over the front of her jeans like a muffin-top. Carter would tell me in private that he liked her boobs. He would say, "I like them titties. I like them titties a lot."

She would put Lynn to bed. When he got tired, Carter would trundle off to bed as well. Sachi then would coax me into staying up and say she would get me something from the corner store just down the street, like an ice cream or sweet cake. She would, too, and bring it back to the house. I would eat it fast before she could take it back. Afterwards, Sachi would just start looking at me funny, sort of with her head down and her eyes looking up. I remember thinking it was kind of cute in a way. She would then get really quiet and slide down her pants and then her underwear, if she were wearing any. Sometimes, she wasn't.

I would see the deep red cris-crossing lines around her stomach where the skin was all bunched up because her pants were too tight. It looked painful. I'd look away because I didn't want to see her naked and also because I knew what was going to happen next.

She would then get on her knees and take down my underwear. Usually, I was wearing only a pair of underwear and an old t-shirt. Sometimes, she would giggle, but mostly she just put her mouth over me and made sucking sounds. The pain was enormous, but I would not cry out. If I did, Carter or

Lynn might come out of their bedrooms. They would see what Sachi was doing and that I was not stopping her.

More strangers. Faceless men and women. Men Mother would bring home from the bar. Women who visited from the neighborhood and drank with Mother. Shoving my hand inside themselves while wiggling on their backs, moaning and laughing at the same time. Their breasts sagging like their bellies. And Mother always within only a few feet away, hidden in some other room. Sometimes she would be with a man and sometimes alone, but she always knew when to come out – after they had finished. When it was all over, she would collect the money. And I saw, she would collect the money from the ladies too.

With the thoughts of Marla still lingering, I was nearly home. By the time I reached our house, I really started to doubt Lauren was going to take us in. As a matter of fact, I never really believed Mother would have let us go without a fight. Not out of love, but out of spite.

"Come here, Gregg!" Mother was standing with her hands firmly against her hips. "Were you and Carter fighting?" she said in her most righteous tone. "I don't tolerate fighting in this house!"

For a long time I did not answer. I just stood there looking at the ground and listening to her breathe really hard through her false teeth. I did not know what to say. There was never a good answer. We were fighting, and if I lied Mother would see right through me. If I told the truth, it would be the same fate. So I just stood there and waited. I waited for what she had already set her mind to do long before I came back from the field.

She continued to stand on the porch with her hands on her hips and staring down at me. The last light of the day was fading. "Get in this goddamn house," she said, turned and walked inside.

I followed her, stopping on the small dirty and peeling square of linoleum just past the door. With what strength I had left in my voice I squeaked out, "I'm sorry, Mamma. We were just wrestling." It was a lie, but panic set in, and it was all I had left.

Lynn was wrapped in an old winter coat and sitting on the floor. Carter was sitting on the couch. Mother stood only inches from me.

"Don't you say another goddamn word," Mother said and grit her teeth so hard I could hear them grind together. "I'm going to beat you black and blue."

"Mom, no," Lynn whimpered.

When Mother grabbed for me, I threw my hands instinctively in front of my face and then let them fall to my side. The life had run from me, and I felt I no longer even had the strength left to protect myself.

Suddenly, she stopped. It was Carter that caused her to pause for a moment by letting out a killer scream that filled the house. It sounded as if the roof had been ripped off. That was all it took for her to change direction and now focus on him. Carter was at an age when he was coming into his own. He just looked at Mother with an expression on his face that was both anger and something that could break your heart. He clenched his fists, and he too grit his teeth. If not for the little beads of sweat at his temples, you'd think he was not afraid, but he was. Mother looked confused as if her only ally betrayed her – like they had some sort of secret bond, and Carter just broke it. Mother then walked to the couch, sat down, and told us all to get out. We quietly filed one by one out the front door. I was filled with relief, but I knew it was only temporary.

When we reached the sidewalk leading to the porch, we heard a loud bang, and the door was shut and locked behind us. Although it was still summer, the nights grew cool. Lynn was still wrapped in the old winter coat. The sleeves dangled empty. Carter and Lynn were not wearing shoes. The three of us stood in the fading orange light, looking at the ground and wondering what to do.

"We'll sit under the awning in the back," Carter said. Again, one by one, we rounded the corner of the house, passing the old wooden gate, and found our places under the awning. We sat on old lawn chairs and at a broken picnic table. We did not speak. There was nothing to say. We just had to wait until Mother let us back inside.

Normally, I would have been peering through the kitchen window in order to check on Mother and make sure she wasn't trying to burn the house down or commit suicide. But at first, it didn't seem to be in me anymore. However, it was still there a little, and I felt the twinge of fear creep inside me and tell me that Mother was probably cutting her wrist right now. Yet I was so tired.

The twinge in my gut told me that at least a part of me was lying. Despite my realization that I could live without her, I still couldn't let go. Although I was tired, I still loved her. It had been eleven years with Mother. It was the love part that forced me to get up and walk to the window on the side of the house and peer in.

I shimmied up the wooden gate and leaned over, bracing myself on the small ledge of the window frame in order to look inside. When I did, my blood ran cold.

Mother was sitting on an old bench behind the kitchen table and facing the window. She was just staring at a knife and turning it slowly in her hand. I went to slam my fist against the glass and plead for her to stop as I had done so many times before, but before I did our eyes met. Mother saw me looking, and it was then she put the point of the knife against her breast. She had been waiting for me. Expecting me to look through the window. The sham was uncovered.

When she saw me just staring and doing nothing to stop her, she threw the knife at me. It clattered against the glass, making me jump and lose my balance. I fell to the ground, and before I could get back up, I heard her angry voice calling me inside.

Carter and Lynn were behind me now and followed as I walked toward the front door. When we rounded the side of the house and turned to walk up the steps of the porch, we saw Mother standing in the doorway.

"Not you two fucking bastards – him," and she pointed her crooked finger at me.

I walked inside and was rendered a hard slap to the back of my head, as a prelude to what lie ahead. Carter and Lynn stood at the bottom of the porch, quietly pleading with their eyes. When Mother slammed the door, I caught a glimpse of Lynn and saw she was crying.

"Take off your clothes . . . all of them."

Mother spoke in a low angry tone, but you could also hear the excitement in her voice.

"No, Mommy," I said, but was already pulling off my shirt.

Mother's face reminded me of Jonny Noost. He was a boy from down the street, who I had once watched stick a pin in a toad's leg. His eyes danced with excitement as the toad limped around. It made me sad when I saw the toad hop and the leg with the pin in it sort of drag behind, trying to catch up.

Mother could not wait, telling me to hurry so I removed the last of my clothing as quickly as I could. I now stared at the carpet, cupping my small genitals.

"Let me see that winkie, you little queer. Let me see what the men suck," she said grinning, and I could see her false teeth were jutting slightly out of her mouth. Then, using a sucking technique, she righted them underneath her gums. Before I could move my hands out of the way, she rendered two rapid slaps to my groin that forced my own hands to slam against my testicles. There was an arc of light that flashed behind my eyes as the pain shot down my legs and then up into my gut like hot lead. I fell to the floor feeling sick and all done in. Drained and worn down, I only wanted the pain to go away and this to be the end.

"You have a little winkie," Mother whispered, now hovering over my body, as I lay curled in a fetal position to one side.

"How can you put that in a woman?"

She then put her arm under my neck and pulled me upward into a sitting position. The room swam and I nearly fell backward again, but she jerked me forward and held me upright.

"Cross your legs like an Indian." Her words swam in and out of my head like the room.

She continued to speak quietly.

"Have you had enough?" she said sweetly.

"Yes," I answered, still reeling from the sickening pain in my belly.

"No. No, Gregg, you haven't."

And with one hand squeezing my shoulder to keep me straight, she reached down with the other and grabbed hold of my penis with her thumb and forefinger. "Move your hands out of the way . . . Mommy is going to see if you're okay."

Her voice never lost that sweet pitch to it, which made it sound even more crazy. She didn't pinch, but instead gently pulled the loose skin forward and backward. It was worse than the hitting and slapping. I pushed her hands away. I could not go through with it.

My defiance enraged Mother. Letting go of my penis, she landed a slap across my face, knocking me backward to the floor. Compared to the rape, the slap actually came as a relief. Again holding my genitals, I rolled to one side. Taking a handful of my hair on the back of my head, Mother twisted my face toward hers with one quick jerk. Leaning into me, our mouths almost touching, Mother whispered, "I'm going to kill you tonight."

I did not say a word. I just kept hoping that she would not touch my genitals again. The alcohol was thick on her breath, pungent and sickening. Our mouths were so close, her breath became my own. My stomach lurched and a puke burp escaped my throat, causing Mother to back away from my face. She stood up kicking me once, telling me to get up and go to bed. I did, and later that evening, when Carter crawled into bed next to me, the shame was so great I pretended to be asleep.

With my eyes squeezed tightly together, I lie very still and awake next to my brother. Minutes later, I listened as Carter's breathing slipped into the familiar pattern of sleep. An hour had gone by, maybe two, and I was still awake. Carter grunted as if dreaming and rolled over. I held my breath and waited for him to settle again. When I felt it was safe to open my eyes, I looked around the dark room and watched the moon shadows dance along the walls and ceiling. I watched with eyes wide open. I watched and waited for Mother.

I did not have to wait for long. Mother came to the door and stood, saying nothing. What little courage I had earlier, to push her hands away, had left me. I understood completely and crawled quietly from the bed not wanting to wake Carter. We walked in silence to her bedroom with me following closely behind. Mother had told me she was going to kill me this night – and in a way she did.

CHAPTER FOURTEEN

THE NEXT AFTERNOON, I hid inside the old closet leading to the attic and smeared lotion on my raw genitals. The lotion stung my penis. I wanted to stay in the closet forever.

There was suddenly movement in the bedroom, and I stopped dead with my hand greasy from lotion, cupping my groin. I was scared to death I would be caught in this position, but I was too afraid to move. Through the rickety door of the closet, through its broken slats, I watched Mother step into the bedroom. I backed up as far as possible, pressing my body against the far wall and continued peering through the slats. Mother was clad only in a pair of worn underwear. Her breasts sagged and were terribly wrinkled. In her hand was a bottle – half-empty. She appeared to be waiting for someone. I kept perfectly still. Seconds later, in walked a stranger.

"Don't fuck with me!" Mother shouted to the man.

"Here! Here's the money!" the man said and forcibly shoved a wad of something in her free hand. His speech was as slurred as Mother's.

Mother set the bottle on an old dresser, and they both fell into bed. I turned and looked away as she pulled off her dirty panties, throwing them to the floor. Afterwards, I could hear them both thrashing around. The man was grunting.

"Hurry up!" Mother demanded, and the man's grunting intensified. I covered my ears with my hands, but could not shut out the noise. My head was bent down, and I saw that I still had not pulled up my underwear. Too afraid to move, I just closed my eyes. Closed them hard. I was faint and fought back a nauseating feeling.

"Get the fuck off me!" Mother said after the man apparently had finished.

"Fucking whore," the man grumbled and pulled on his pants.

There was an exchange of curses from both of them, and the man left the room. I could hear him push past the battered front screen door which banged hard against the side of the house. A car door slammed. Then, there was the sound of a car driving off, and soon afterwards, Mother shouted to the room, "I've been raped!"

Despite the hint of false terror in her slurred words, had I not been in the closet, I may have believed her. I would have at least tried. It would have been easier to do so. Knowing she was lying made what had just taken place much worse.

I sat perfectly still. Too afraid to make a sound, I knew if Mother found me in the closet with the lotion and my genitals exposed, she would beat me into unconsciousness, accusing me of spying on her sex act with the man. I waited, and although it seemed like hours instead of minutes, Mother finally left the room. I watched as she slipped back into her underwear, grabbed the bottle off the dresser, and staggered out of the room.

I listened and heard Mother finish dressing in the living room. Where she had allowed the man to undress her, not caring if her children walked in on them. I listened until I heard her walk through the kitchen and then out the back door. I heard the scrape of metal against concrete as she fell into the lawn chair under the awning in the backyard. I listened. Leaned forward and nearly vomited, and then, I listened some more.

Pulling on my underwear and a pair of Carter's too big for me hand-me-down swim trunks, I gently opened the closet door and slid off the small platform, and down onto the bedroom floor. The room smelled of sex and decay. The man's cologne hung in the air and mixed with the smell of Mother's scent. A scent I could no longer seem to wash completely off my hands.

Quickly walking from the bedroom, I made a beeline for the front door in the opposite direction of where Mother was in the backyard. Before leaving the house, I popped on my tennis shoes near the door, not bothering to try and tie the laces. I wore an old tank top and no socks. Standing in our front yard, I could hear the faint musical sound of the ice-cream truck one block over behind Kyle's house. It would be rounding the corner soon and my empty stomach grumbled in protest.

Kyle was in his front yard setting up their sprinkler and waved for me to come over and I crossed the street. The temperature was screaming hot, and I thought the water would feel good, especially on my sore genitals from Mother's rough sex the night before. Kyle turned the squeaky water faucet counter-clockwise until it would not turn any more. There was a low groan from the exterior of the house, and the hose attached to the sprinkler swelled. Then came a hissing sound as a horizontal row of holes across a silver oscillating arm suddenly shot thin streams of water into the air. Both Kyle and I screeched with delight.

Bracing for the cold water, Kyle and I were readying ourselves to sprint through the vertical threadlike jets, when the ice-cream truck came lumbering down the street clanging loudly. Mrs. Jacobson surprised us by coming outside and offered up a whole dollar for Kyle and I to share for ice-cream. In no time at all, Kyle and I, red-faced and already getting sunburned, were standing shy of a few other kids at the window where the man in white would exchange the dollar for treats.

I remember Kyle handing the man the dollar and quickly shoving the change in his trunks, and I remember the ice cream cone I got, but not the flavor. Then I shot around the front of the truck, having only licked the cone maybe once, and a car that had been driving past the truck hit me. It clipped my left arm, the one holding on to the ice cream cone, and spun me around like a top.

I forgot all about the ice-cream that went flying out of my hand and landed someplace a great distance from where I was standing. I hardly remember the car hitting me, but I remember the suddenness of it and wailing like a banshee. And how I almost passed out right in the middle of the street, cradling my left arm that already felt twice as big as my right.

All that I had wanted was to eat the ice-cream before it melted. Before my siblings saw I had gotten one. Before Mother had seen, most of all. I hadn't bothered to look before running into the street and had not seen the car until after it struck my arm. The sound of tires screeching did not register in my mind until afterwards. Until after the earth began to spin much faster, and then, there was the hot ache in my left arm, and the earth went on spinning.

The driver had stopped and jumped from the car and ran to me while I slowly pulled myself up in the bright June light. He was frantically feeling my body and apologizing. He looked very afraid, and his head kept darting around as if trying to find someone. I ran from him crying and toward our house. I do not know when Mother had come from the backyard, but she was now standing on the porch. She did not run to me, only stood there.

When I bolted past her, she moved slightly and let me go inside. From inside the living room, I heard the driver just outside the front door apologizing to Mother. She mumbled something and he left. Mother came inside the house. I was sitting on the loveseat holding my arm and trying very hard to stop crying. She told me to lie down, and I did. On my back, I let my badly swollen arm lay across my chest giving myself a one-arm hug. It felt heavy.

The sun was going down, leaving slanted shadows of purple light across the living room, giving it a sense of summer shade. I tried to will the fingers of my swollen arm open, but the pain was too great, causing me to writhe, and white light flooded my brain. I was within an inch of screaming and bit down hard, sucking in air through my clenched teeth. The tears ran from my eyes, slipping down my cheeks and into my ears, tickling and making them pop. I never imagined I could sleep with pain like this, but I was wrong, and soon I fell blissfully asleep.

When I woke, Mother sat in a chair, regarding me coldly over a lit cigarette, holding a glass of wine. Carter and Lynn sat side-by-side in another chair with worried faces.

Carter spoke. "You were hit by a car."

Sharp stabs of pain pricked at my left arm.

Lynn was talking now. "Gregg, you were hit by a car."

Then I was falling asleep again. Going. Going away from the room. Mother was still watching me and smoking. Quiet. Too quiet. Lynn was crying. Carter looked worried. I was listening to the wind outside. It sounded like blowing rain. Lynn was talking. Talking. Talking. The drummer in my head beating louder. Mother sitting and staring, smoking one cigarette after another, drinking. And then everything was blotted out.

Again, I awoke. I was so hot. Turning my head slightly toward her, I saw Mother get up from her chair and walk over to me. She balanced a glass of wine in one hand while a cigarette jutted from her fingers. It struck me odd both the glass and cigarette were in her left hand. *She's right-handed*, I thought and again went away. Falling. Falling.

I was drifting in and out of sleep, and when I awoke again, Mother was kneeling next to the loveseat. She rubbed my leg with her right hand and looked into my face. Suddenly, she turned toward where Carter and Lynn were sitting and sent them to bed. They left the room and waved when passing by. I watched them go and took a deep breath. My swollen arm, still lying across my chest, moved and felt as if it would split open.

"Your arm is just bruised," Mother said, smiling, and I saw the lipstick caked between her teeth. It looked like blood. She got up and looked toward the bedrooms. Waited a moment, then turned, and knelt down beside me once again. Placing her glass on the floor, she casually plopped her cigarette into what was left of the wine, which produced a short hissing sound.

Mother then unexpectedly cupped the hand that once held her glass firmly over my mouth. With her other hand, she gripped my swollen arm and squeezed hard. I recall the taste of tobacco on her palm, and then there was nothing but pain. Pain followed by peace. Falling. Falling, and then finally gone.

CHAPTER FIFTEEN

AS THE WEEKS WENT ON, our interaction with Kyle, Louis, and Alexis dwindled down to almost nothing. We rarely ever saw them, even though they lived right across the street from us. On one level, the isolation bit deep and left me angry, but there was also the relief of hiding away and not having them see me. The older I got, the more aware of my situation I became and the more ashamed. As I grew older, shame turned into rage. The more I thought about the abuse, especially the sex, the more the rage built up inside me. It strangled me and clawed at my skin.

Kyle's parents stopped their children from even playing at our house. Mrs. Jacobson, once warm and friendly, now seemed distant and cold to me, Carter, and Lynn. Mr. Jacobson was no longer tender and polite. He seemed cold as well.

We were giving up. Mother was cutting away at our will to live. Even Carter began to lose weight at an alarming rate. His clothes, once snug, now hung loose. We wore our poverty in plain view and did not try to hide it any longer. We were victims of Mother's great and terrible energy. We were alone with a monster in the house, and every moment with her became a fight to get my breath back. I missed playing with Kyle. Time spent was always with Mother, and the best of these times was when she was not a monster or a mother – the best times were when she was asleep. But this was no longer enough.

I was alone in the backyard. "One more time she beats you," that's what Jessica had said. "One more time, and I'll come and take you away from her."

Jessica would have taken us away that same day if I had broken down right there on the spot when she made her promise. However, I was a child and thought like a child. I took her words literally and believed I had to wait for that one more time. In addition, I had grown so used to hiding my feelings away that I couldn't come totally clean with her. It would have meant telling her everything. I could have told her about the beatings, but not the sex. I just wasn't able to do that.

Another part of me felt that even telling Jessica about the worst of the beatings would not have been enough to convince her. I had grown so used to the lies that I was afraid if Jessica did not see fresh blood from some ragged, wandering gash across my face, she was never going to help us. I had been beaten repeatedly since Jessica's promise, but I did not call her. I just couldn't get up the nerve.

I was in the backyard standing next to the lilac bush. It was in full bloom and normally I would have taken in the exotic scent and found it both pleasing and relaxing. Instead, the smell rose up in my nose and filled my throat, making me gag and eventually vomit.

As I stared at the fresh pool of vomit on the grass near the lilac bush, I knew I had to draw the beating. I knew it was time.

My nerves were on edge, and I vomited again while hanging on to the cyclone fence that separated our yard from the neighbors. I recall thinking dully that I hoped they were not home. Another dry heave told me there was nothing left to throw up. I buckled over from the gut-wrenching act and folded my arms across my belly. Then, standing up slowly, I unfolded my arms and let them dangle by my side. Breathing in and out deeply, I reached inside the front pocket of my pants and felt the two dimes I had been saving to call Jessica. I turned and abruptly started for the back door.

I'm going to do it, I said to myself. *I'm going to make her mad and draw the beating.* I went into the house. It seemed the only thing left to do, and even then, I waited for something to stop me. A sign of sorts that would tell me I didn't have to do this. Nothing came. Only Mother was in the living room. Carter and Lynn were not home. Now only the two of us. Again. Mother was leaning to one side of the couch and mumbling when she saw me. My eyes were fixed on her. She made no pretense of listening to what I was saying.

"Mom, why do you drink?" I said again. This time louder and still just above a whisper. I had no breath left in me. My mouth was dry, and it quivered. She heard this time. I could tell by the way she stopped mumbling and stared right through me. I panicked and nearly took it all back. Almost begged for mercy and recanted what I just said, but it was too late.

"What the fuck did you just say?" she asked abruptly. I stood silent, looking down at the floor.

"How dare you question me!" Her voice squeaked when it reached an unbelievable pitch, quavering just a bit. She was in utter disbelief and still trying to get her mind around the question. Moreover, the fact I would ask it in the first place. It was the perfect question, and one that came to me only after entering the room seconds before. I knew it would cut deeper than any other.

"Come here, you little cocksucker!" She was literally shaking with anger, ready to explode. At first, she only sat on the couch, screaming at the floor. Suddenly, she stopped screaming, looked directly at my face, and glared. Then unexpectedly, in one smooth and fluid motion, Mother lunged, clearing the coffee table and hitting my chest with full force.

I fell backward, and my body smacked the floor, absorbing our combined weights. There was a quick flash of light and the sound of rushing air escaping my lungs. Straddling my body, Mother positioned herself directly above me, slapping at my face. With every slap, light and dark wrestled with one another behind my eyes as if watching a torch fall down a long dark well. We were crotch to crotch, Mother bending forward slightly, while she continued slapping at my face. Left and right. Back and forth. Over and over. Every now and again, raking her cigarette-stained nails across my cheeks. I felt the scratches on my skin and both Mother and I were sweating. The sweat ran into the fresh scratches, making them sting and causing a deeper ache.

Thankfully, Carter came home, and seeing Mother, he shouted for her to get off me. His voice was harsh and throaty. Standing bent over and directly behind her, he then immediately locked his arms around her small shoulders and tried to pull her off. Mother instantly snapped her head back, rendering Carter a solid butt to the nose, causing Carter to squeal in pain. A covet of blood shot from his nostrils and onto Mother's back.

Carter continued to shout and pull at Mother, turning his face from side to side in an attempt to avoid more of her head butts. "Run!" he shouted.

Mother's weight kept me pinned down with my arms locked to my side, and I could not move. Carter lunged backward while holding tightly on to Mother and managed to pull her off me.

"Run!" Carter shouted again.

This time I managed to wiggle free, and knowing he could not hold her for long, I desperately struggled to stand. I managed to pull myself to my feet, hung my head over them until the world swam back into focus, then half-staggered, half-crawled to the front door.

Once outside, the sun burned the cuts on my face, and my head was throbbing. I looked toward the corner where the pay phone was. *I can't make it,* I thought and started to cry. I dropped to one knee and tried to catch my breath. I knelt in the yard for a moment, gathering myself, and then rose to a standing position. I again headed for the pay phone.

Suddenly, through the haze of pain, I heard Mother burst through the screen door. I turned just in time to meet her wide-open gaze.

"Get the fuck back in here!" she shouted.

This got me moving again. I headed toward the corner store as quickly as I could.

Mother shouted threats, and I heard them even as I crossed the street at the end of our block. I remember looking both ways, but could not see because of the tears standing in my eyes and they were nowhere near letting up. So, as best I could, I hurriedly crossed and hoped a car would not come along and hit me. I reached the edge of the small parking lot, and on unsteady legs, I walked over to the bright silver *Bell* pay phone.

Sobbing violently, I reached inside the pocket of my pants and was immediately filled with dread. The dimes were gone. I tried the other pocket. Nothing. I again switched to the pocket I was sure I had placed the dimes earlier that morning. On a few occasions, I had come close to spending them on sweets, and even though my stomach gnawed at itself when thinking about it, I did not.

After shoving both my hands as hard as I could into both my front pockets at the same time, I finally happened upon the dimes. They were in the pocket I had placed them originally. With unsteady fingers, I dropped the first dime into the slot and dialed Jessica's number. She answered. My throat locked and I could not make a sound. She hung up after saying hello two, maybe three times.

One dime remained for one more call. Dropping the second and last dime I had into the slot, I dialed carefully, and Jessica answered again, obviously irritated by a crank caller. I managed a few broken words and then heard only silence, followed by dial tone.

Placing the phone back into its cradle, I gathered what strength I had left. While clutching at the air in order to breathe, I walked to the rear of the store where there was a garden hose attached to the building. The keeper used it to rinse the small asphalt parking lot. Not caring if the keeper came outside, I turned the knob and waited for the water to gush from the nozzle. There was a bad moment when the water did not come, but then eventually it did. After a whoosh of air followed by a few spits of spray, a steady stream of water began to run from the hose. I waited as the water went from warm to cool. Holding the hose, I watched the clear water rush past and brought it carefully to my lips. I drank greedily. I drank the cold water until my belly cramped.

To ease the pain in my beaten-up face, I splashed a handful of cool water over it. Afterwards, I turned the faucet clockwise until it locked into place. I thought for sure the keeper would come running from his store as soon as he heard the high-pitched squeal of the water being pinched off in the pipe. He did not. I dropped the hose, which made a hollow clinking sound on the asphalt, and began to walk toward home.

I slowly walked past the silver *Bell* pay phone and over the small square of asphalt that made up the parking lot of the corner store that was only able to fit maybe three or four cars at the most. Across the street and past the first three ticky-tacky houses, and there I stopped. I stopped short of a line of shrubs and hid, peering around just enough to catch a glimpse of Mother still standing on the porch. Not sitting. Standing. She was intent on finishing this.

Lynn must have come home while I was at the pay phone calling Jessica. I watched Carter and Lynn walking away from the house and toward me. When they got closer, I stepped slightly into view so they could see me.

"Mom wants you home," Carter said.

I saw in his face that he was just delivering the message, but did not feel it should be honored. His nose looked twice its normal size and it was beet red. There was dried blood on his chin and the front of his shirt. Carter's blue eyes were wet and shiny.

"Mom said we're both in big trouble," Carter said.

I figured he avoided a beating for holding her down just long enough to come and fetch me. I was pretty sure he was going to pay later.

Lynn was by his side. "Tell me we're going away, Gregg," Lynn said, and the tears ran down her cheeks. "Tell me!" she pleaded, and I broke from the weight of regret. My plan failed. Believing the call never got through to Jessica, I was consumed by remorse and took my anger out on Lynn.

I replied, "Fuck you!" – and immediately felt the terrible weight of even more guilt for responding this way.

Lynn recoiled from the outburst, but stayed next to Carter. Still hidden by the shrub, the three of us waited. By the time Jessica's familiar car rounded the corner behind us, we were all weeping uncontrollably.

CHAPTER SIXTEEN

JESSICA ROLLED TO THE CURB and from the car told us to meet her at the house. With one look, she knew whatever had happened had started with Mother. I wiped the snot from my nose, and the three of us started walking home. When Jessica turned into the driveway, Mother darted in the house. We watched as Jessica got out of her car, walking briskly and bent-over with her fists pumping back and forth as she went. She strode with a purpose, and I was filled with a mixture of joy, terror, and sorrow.

By the time the three of us walked into the house, Jessica had Mother pinned down on the couch, and it looked like she was choking her with her own collar. Mother just looked up at Jessica, as if in some sort of stupor, and pretended she did not understand what was going on. I do not remember all of what Jessica said, but I do recall it involved a lot of cursing. Mother just sat there the whole time, quiet, watching Jessica's face. Every now and then Jessica would pop Mother in the mouth with her hand, and I would flinch. That was the first time I saw Mother take guff from anyone. Dad was ten times Jessica's size and Mother would fight him. However, she did not fight Jessica. Mother appeared to be somewhat afraid, but mostly docile and shockingly apologetic. It looked like all the fight had finally gone from her – as if she had finally ran out of all the hate that made her strong all these years.

Then Mother just started laughing with this detached look on her face. Carter, Lynn, and I just stood off to the side and watched with confused horror. None of us knew what to do, and I was actually afraid for her. I was relieved when Jessica finally let go of Mother's shirt, but then suddenly, with split-second timing, Jessica hauled off and landed a hard slap across Mother's face.

"Don't hurt her!" I screamed.

Afterwards, I was afraid Jessica would get mad at me for sticking up for Mother and just leave, but she did not. Instead, she just kept yelling at Mother, letting loose all those things pent up inside her for far too long.

Many of the things Jessica said I had already heard from my older sisters – usually right before they stormed from the house for the last time. However, some of the things Jessica was saying I had not heard. Some of the accusations I wish I had never heard. Like how Father had raped Jessica and Lauren, and how Mother had allowed this to take place. That made me think of the stranger – and Mother in the next room, laughing when I passed by.

Jessica told us to go outside and wait in the car. I pleaded with her again not to hurt Mother. She did not respond to my plea, instead just said that she would be right behind us. Silently, my siblings and I walked from the house. I did not realize it would be the last time.

Carter went first, followed by Lynn, then me. I was staring at Mother the entire time. We descended the crumbling steps of the porch and into a thick smell of gasoline coming from Jessica's old car motor that was still running. We climbed inside the backseat, and I watched the day end its life through a stained red sun slipping beneath the horizon.

We waited anxiously for Jessica while I secretly hoped she would not hurt Mother. Minutes that seemed like hours went by, and Jessica finally came outside. She climbed behind the wheel of the car and put it into gear. As we backed out of the driveway, Mother walked outside and stood on the porch, folding her arms as she did. I breathed a sigh of relief and heard Carter do the same. The car swung into the street, and Jessica changed gears. Mother smiled, lifting an arm to wave as we drove away.

From the backseat of the car, in between Carter and Lynn, I turned and faced out the back window as we continued to drive away. Mother was still standing on the porch and waving. I slowly lifted my hand and waved back. We rounded the corner, and she was gone.

Now facing forward, I stared down at a pair of hand-me-down shoes, much too large for my feet. Laces undone and hanging past the worn rubber soles. It was dusk, shadows were thickening, and I could see the first face of a bloated moon. My cheeks burned from the cuts left by Mother's nails.

Beside me, Lynn is crying. Carter stares out the window. I attempt to speak but cannot find my voice. My throat is hard and dry. Jessica looks at me in the rearview mirror, shakes her head in disgust, and then turns her eyes back on the road. On we drive toward Jessica's, where the next day we will leave with Lauren. Behind me is a past that is still not done. Behind me is Mother. Alone.

We drive without speaking to one another. I struggle to gather up all the force I have left to fight the impending panic that threatens to suffocate me. The day's events rush in and out of my mind. I try and cast them aside, only to have each ugly event come back even stronger than before. I examine what I've done and start crying. Jessica pulls the car over and drags me from it. I can only stop crying long enough to choke up the vomit that had been boiling in the pit of my belly.

Back in the car, I'm freezing. I roll into a ball and try to become invisible between Carter and Lynn.

As we drive further away from Mother's, the air seems to soften. I speak, but uneasily now. Stomach acid stings the back of my throat, and I have to keep swallowing to ease the pain. We pass more tacky houses and eventually the railway tracks, then on to the highway. The windows are down, and a warm wind blows. Holding my face up toward the open car window, I let the wind dry my eyes and breathe in slowly.

We hurry faster down the highway. Picking up speed. Jessica wants to get home. She wants this night to be over. The moon is blurred by passing clouds. I'm growing more anxious. We hurry.

The warm wind blows. Inside me, there is something familiar stirring. Longing. I now know what it is. At last, it comes to me while we hurry away.

I want to go home. Mother needs me.

The thought passed with mixed emotion. I realized that Mother had been at the root of my devotion, but that sentiment has begun to leave me and will eventually fall away for good.

For the first time in eleven years, the heavy curtain of abuse has been raised, lifting a long awaited veil of hope – and showing me the possibilities of a *beautiful world*.

DEAR READER

IT IS TRUE THAT I PUSH ON. It is also true that I have met, and hope to continue meeting, some of the most wonderful people in a world that can be beautiful – at times. I will also tell you that I keep expecting the demons left inside of me from the abuse to take over once and for all. They are worse in the nightmares I am plagued with, and I often wake up trying to catch my breath. Sometimes, I lay there and work through them. Sometimes, I go into the bathroom and cry and swear I can still smell Mother and feel her fingers.

There's all this terror filled up in me, and it seems that it will never go away. Even now, I have to bite down hard on all those feelings remembering giving in to several perverse things because I did not know any better or I loved someone. A love that is more like doom when you're that little and that young and stupid. Sometimes, I gave in because I was scared or because it was blood. A father. A mother and son.

I don't know what really brought on the horror of Mother and Father. I have thought about why sometimes parents hurt their own children and how people can make a child do terrible things. I think about that a lot, and I will never figure that out. Ever.

If you were kind enough to read this book, I will let you in on another secret. Softer than velvet this fear slips in and out of me. I don't want to be afraid of it, and I'm not, most of the time, but I keep thinking of what Mother left inside me and wonder if maybe it's in me still. The nightmares aren't always Mother doing terrible things, sometimes it's me and it's to the people I love and who love me back. Also, I don't want to cry, but I think it would be a relief if I could really cry hard while someone held me, but in my forties I am still too ashamed to ask.

Writing this book has brought back a lot of scary memories. The worst of them were still left out of the book. There were just so many. As an adult, I slip every now and then and fear I have been marked for later by something lurking behind the terrible things in my mind. A darkness that waits until I am too old to work and preoccupy myself. Too old and feeble to fight it. I wonder if you know what I mean. I believe you do.

Perhaps by writing this book and telling these things, it gave me just enough relief to keep me from letting the bad stuff get to me. Perhaps that's part of the healing – the telling part that helps sweep away the bad things. I do not know. What I do know is that I tried and I am still trying. I will not quit. It is my anchor that holds me in place, so the world (sometimes ugly…sometimes beautiful) does not bowl me over. It is my anchor keeping me in place waiting for you.

LaVergne, TN USA
13 October 2010
200724LV00001B/23/P